HANNIE RAYSON is a graduate of Melbourne University and the Victorian College of the Arts (VCA) and has an Honorary Doctorate of Letters from La Trobe University. A co-founder of Theatreworks, she has served as writer-in-residence at the Mill Theatre, Playbox Theatre, La Trobe University, Monash University and VCA. Her theatre credits include *Please Return to Sender* (1980) and *Mary* (1981), each premiering at Theatreworks; and *Leave It Till Monday* (1984), which was first produced by the Mill Theatre. *Room to Move* (1985) won the Australian Writers' Guild AWGIE Award for Best Original Stage Play.

Her next play, *Hotel Sorrento* (1990), a Playbox / Theatreworks co-production, won an AWGIE Award as well as a NSW Premier's Literary Award and Green Room Award for Best Play of 1990. *Falling From Grace* (1994), winner of a NSW Premier's Literary Award and the *Age* Performing Arts Award, also premiered at Playbox, as did *Competitive Tenderness* (1996).

Life After George (2000) opened at MTC and went on to win the Victorian Premier's Literary Award, the Green Room Award for Best New Australian Play, and Best New Australian Work at the 2001 Helpmann Awards. It became the first play to be nominated for the Miles Franklin Award.

Her plays have been performed extensively around Australia and a number have been produced overseas.

Hannie's television scripts include *Sloth* (ABC, *Seven Deadly Sins*) and co-writing two episodes of *SeaChange* (ABC/Artists Services). A feature film of *Hotel Sorrento*, produced in 1995, was nominated for ten Australian Film Institute Awards. In 1999 she received the Magazine Publishers' Society of Australia's Columnist of the Year Award for her regular contributions to *HQ* magazine.

*Steve Bisley as Lyle in the 2003 Melbourne Theatre Company
production. (Photo: Jeff Busby)*

Inheritance
HANNIE RAYSON

Currency Press, Sydney

CURRENCY PLAYS

Inheritance first published in 2003
by Currency Press Pty Ltd,
PO Box 2287, Strawberry Hills, NSW, 2012, Australia
enquiries@currency.com.au
www.currency.com.au

NATIONAL LIBRARY OF AUSTRALIA CIP DATA
   Rayson, Hannie, 1957–.
      Inheritance.
      Rev. ed.
      ISBN 0 86819 720 3.
      1. Inheritance and succession – Australia – Drama. I. Title.
   A822.3

Publication of this title was assisted by the Commonwealth
Government through the Australia Council, its arts funding
and advisory body.

Set by Dean Nottle.
Cover design by Kate Florance, Currency Press.
Cover shows Lois Ramsey, Steve Bisley and Monica Maughan. Cover
photograph by Earl Carter and design by Garry Emery Design.
Currency Press acknowledges the Traditional Owners of the Country on which we
live and work. We pay our respects to all Aboriginal and Torres Strait Islander
Elders, past and present.

Foreword

Peter Sommerfeld

Sitting in the dark of the Sydney Opera House, experiencing *Inheritance* for the first time, was an intensely personal journey. It was set in the district where I was raised in the 1940s and 1950s. Names of little Mallee towns came at me from the stage, couched in dialogue with true vernacular and performed with perfect cadence. Chinkapook, Wycheproof, Swan Hill, Nyah West. Hannie took me home.

These were all places I'd go to regularly with Pop, my grandfather, fifty years ago in his old truck, to fossick in their council rubbish tips collecting bottles, old batteries, copper wire, which he'd later sell. He was the town's bottle-oh. My grandmother archly insisted on the term second-hand or marine dealer but he was happy with the other handle. These were the people who raised me after my mother died and my dad joined up in 1941.

I stopped going out with Pop once I hit eleven or twelve, when I was far too cool to be seen doing that sort of thing any more. But secretly I still ached to be there with him, out on those clear winter mornings on the road to Lalbert, rollie stuck to his bottom lip, ash falling down his shirt front as he sang 'I'll Take You Home Again, Kathleen'. Turning to me mid-chorus, 'Might stop for a coupla quickies at the Royal in Quambatook, all right? I'll bring you out a lemon squash, okay? An' Ol' Missus... whassername? Ol' Missus Fiddlearse at the store? She'll prob'ly 'ave some empties to pick up. An' keep Sport in the cabin when I pull up so he don' bite no bugger. Orright?'

Like thousands of other post-war, smart-arse, working-class kids I was offered another road. Secondary schooling, higher education, independence and eventually all those middle-class trappings we'd all coveted in 1940s American movies. All this and the influence of an emerging youth culture created the gulf that alienated many of us from our working-class roots. In my case (and I've considered this frequently because of my sexuality) I wonder what would have happened if I'd stayed. What was the likelihood of becoming yet another statistic of the rural suicides so devastatingly underlined in *Inheritance*? Tragedies far too frequent still in the case of rural gay youth, yet, strangely, seldom acknowledged as a significant factor in statistics.

Yet virtually forced to abandon my roots, I know I lost something extremely precious, or at least buried something of intrinsic value. And for me this was the power of *Inheritance*. Predominantly it evoked an enormous sense of loss. The loss of my mob; the loss of the ancient river gums that are slowly dying; native fish choked by carp; native animals and birds prey to feral species; paddocks ruined by salination. But most of all, the loss of the open-hearted, 'fair go' attitude engendered by my grandparents and others like them, who'd experienced the real horrors of the Depression. It's to my grave disillusionment that some of their descendents now mouth the poison of Hanson, Howard and Ruddock.

It's through Hannie's diligent, up-front research that she is able to engage us so effectively. She does it again in *Inheritance*—artfully and with great humour. She again takes us through extremely tricky territory, particularly for middle Australia, but the audience stays with her, because she is able to demonstrate the real complexities of these characters, exposing their light and dark and thereby avoiding the far too common patronising stereotype. They truly live for us. We know them. For these reasons we recognise, celebrate and applaud the truth and the great heart in her work.

For those who missed the wonderful original production of *Inheritance* mounted by Melbourne Theatre Company, read on.

Sydney
June 2003

Contents

Speaking Truth to Power:
Hannie Rayson's 'Inheritance'

Hilary Glow

Like Elvis Presley, Pauline Hanson might have left the building, but it's hard to tell for certain. There are periodic sightings around the country and with each appearance she seems increasingly phantasmagorical. But speculations about her corporeality really don't matter, what does matter is counting the cost of the political legacy that has been left behind. There can be no doubt that the emotional and philosophical priorities of One Nation have continued to shape the contemporary political scene. Guy Rundle points out that on the question of political philosophy, Hanson and John Howard share a fundamental view about the importance of racial and cultural homogeneity and, he argues, these 'accorded with the view of an essentially Australian character on which Howard's values [are] grounded'.[1] These essentialist values about Australia and Australian-ness are part of the grab bag of conservative 'common sense' ideas which win votes and help to shape the ideological terrain we inhabit.

Hannie Rayson's *Inheritance* bursts into this cosy conservative world view with so much verve and punch, and with such dramatic flair, that it serves to remind us why theatre (admittedly all too rarely) is a powerful vehicle for the dissenting view. Edward Said has said that the role of the public intellectual is to 'speak truth to power'[2] and this above all else is Rayson's objective. Like all of her plays, *Inheritance* shows Rayson's fascination with understanding those ideas which belong to the category of the apparently self-explanatory ('that's just the way the

---

[1] Guy Rundle, 'The Opportunist: John Howard and the Triumph of Reaction', *Quarterly Essay*, QE 3 2001, p. 26.

[2] Edward Said, 'The Public Role of Writers and Intellectuals' in *The Public Intellectual* (ed.) Helen Small, Blackwell Publishers, Oxford 2002, p.25.

world is'), and asks us to re-think them. And in the process of doing so audiences may find themselves questioning the 'merciless logic' of political power.[3] In *Life After George* (2001), Rayson trained her gaze on the corporatisation of the universities and the concomitant clash between the goals of a liberal education, on the one hand, and economic rationalism's relentless pursuit of the bottom line, on the other. In this new play, Rayson looks at the land, the country we inhabit, and asks: to whom does it belong? Here, there is a whole polyphony of dissonant voices: the two eighty-year-old women, Dibs and Girlie, who have an inherited loyalty to their land, a loyalty which is generations old; the white farmer, Lyle, who struggles to earn a decent living out of his patch of dirt while feeling all the while a crushing disappointment and resentment; Nugget, the adopted Aboriginal son whose sense of belonging (both spiritual and material) is utterly extinguished by an exclusionary white world; Julia and Felix, the city folk who bring to the country their well-intentioned but risibly inappropriate urban values with them in their overnight bags, and are treated like visitors from another planet (planet Melbourne).

Inheritance is a story of two families battling it out in the unforgiving terrain of Victoria's Mallee region. The elderly twin sisters, Dibs Hamilton and Girlie Delaney, represent two kinds of rural family story. Dibs inherited the family farm and has prospered; her children, Julia and William, are well educated city folk, and her adopted Aboriginal son, Nugget, is a successful farmer managing the family farm. Girlie, on the other hand, has had a tougher ride. Her son Lyle and his wife Maureen are embittered by their experience of life on the farm as one of endless struggle and never getting an even break. This group of characters gather together to thrash out (one way or another) the question of who will inherit the family farm, Allandale. The farm has both a literal and metaphorical connotation. Here the 'farm' is a synecdoche for the 'nation'; in other words the part stands for the whole. Along the way Rayson re-writes our grand cultural assumptions about the country and the people who live there. This play takes our often unexamined bush nostalgia, and the endless celebration of the earthy Australian values that are supposedly engendered there, and asks us to look again to find

---

[3] Ibid p.32.

a more complex and disturbing truth. The Hanson/Howard essentialist view of the matey, self-reliant, fair-go Australian is here revealed as a cobbled together rationalization of an altogether more malevolent intolerance of the outsider. This is Rayson's terrain, her métier; all of her plays are explorations of the point at which dominant ideas meet lived experience, and in the explosion of contradictions that this produces, lies the drama.

Inheritance was born out of Rayson's simultaneous curiosity about the social and political world, and her rejection of the black and white dichotomies and taken-for-granted ideas that characterize much contemporary public debate—the sort of thinking, for example, that has allowed the notion of 'political correctness' to enter public discourse both as a derogatory term and a self-evident truth. This play has its genesis in a critical enquiry about the use and currency of 'political correctness' as a strategy for creating consent and tacit approval; it questions the appeal and political successes of One Nation, and the way Hanson's rise to power had managed to produce (and was itself produced by) a great divide in the population. There were the rural 'rednecks' and the urban elites, and the two worlds missed each other by a country mile.

> The sort of rhetoric that both sides were using was at an impasse, a terrible despairing impasse—that was how I experienced it. It just became futile and defeating to keep saying 'what's wrong with these people?' Like most people in my particular circle of family and friends, I was furious and frustrated by Pauline Hanson and her escalating power base and so there was really no alternative for me but to go and find out where that support was coming from, rather than simply saying—those people must be a sandwich short of a picnic.

In order to move beyond this 'despairing impasse', Rayson has peopled *Inheritance* with characters who do not simply reproduce or represent the dichotomous positions of city-vs-country. Rather, the audience looks with fresh eyes at a familiar world made up of characters and scenarios which are readily identifiable, but complex at the same time; we recognize who these people are, we connect to their hopes and aspirations and we feel terribly implicated by both their actions and omissions.

Rayson wants a theatre in which audiences are challenged to look again at what they believe, to think again, to walk into the theatre with one set of ideas and walk out with another. In this regard Rayson might be viewed as an idealist but this is, arguably, the kind of politically-charged, critical optimism that the Australian theatre needs in order to ensure its viability and relevance. Rayson is occasionally accused of writing 'issue' plays; and *Inheritance* was seen by some as a catalogue of contemporary concerns.[4] But the play is more skilful than this, and it avoids the sort of propagandist outcomes that are usually associated with the 'issue' play; a genre Rayson has typified as 'corridor theatre':

> You get to the theatre and you know with a sinking heart that for two hours you'll be walking down a corridor which you can see, at the outset, has a sign that says 'No more freeways for Melbourne', or 'Ban Uranium'… I try to be as surprising and unpredictable as possible because that's the stuff of the drama. So you are not just seeing some sort of values clarification exercise, or illumination of a moral fable, or an inventory of 'issues'. Hopefully, you are so embroiled in the story and captivated by the characters, it is only the next morning over breakfast that certain 'issues' take shape in your mind and open themselves for further consideration.

In creating a complex, dynamic and provocative dramatic experience, one of Rayson's key dramaturgical strategies is the use of contradiction. Dibs is a Christian woman who believes in doing the right thing. In adopting Nugget as her son, for example, Dibs is certain that she is fulfilling her moral responsibilities. And yet, as the play unfolds, it becomes apparent that Dibs is capable of terrible moral perfidy rationalised by her unexamined racism. By creating characters who are not simply black or white but full of contradictions, Rayson not only creates a reality 'effect' in her drama (this is, after all, what people are like), but explores the full spectrum and all the subtle shades of moral ambiguity.

---

[4] Helen Thomson, 'Inheriting the politics of fear and envy', *Age*, 7 March 2003, p.4.

When I say my work is character-driven it means that the plays are always peopled with characters who contain huge contradictions, as do we all, and I am always interested in their having surprising kinds of qualities. People who are ruthless bastards in the board room are very charming at dinner parties, and people who work for the UN or help sink wells in Borneo can be extremely nasty to their own mothers in Bentleigh... the characters themselves have to contain multitudes. I am very taken with that Walt Whitman poem: 'Do I contradict myself? / Very well then I contradict myself, / I am large, I contain multitudes'. I think that's also in itself a kind of politicizing idea—that people are capable of multiple thinking, and they can often sit with contradictory world views.

The dramaturgical emphasis on contradiction emerges most clearly in *Inheritance* as it plays out an intensely personal drama against the socio-political context. One defines and articulates the other. The personal, familial drama of the Hamiltons and the Delaneys, for example, has a sweeping and tragic resonance precisely because we understand these people's story within the framework of colonialism, globalisation and endemic racism. All of this is finely reflected in the story of Nugget's adoption by the Hamiltons whose treatment of their Aboriginal son is marked by a deadly mixture of ignorance, repression, silence and guilt— all thinly papered-over by good intentions. Nugget's story of dispossession speaks volumes about Australia's white history and the difficulty we have in acknowledging not only our racist past but its continuing legacy.

There is a scene at the end of the play where Nugget rakes over his past and his relationship with his father, Farley, who had been his champion... and treated him like a son, but Nugget comes to realize that wasn't enough. One of the major themes in this play is about the white silencing of our history, and how that has completely and utterly disempowered Aboriginal people. I wanted to show that, and to underline it and ram it home. We see that the rug is pulled from underneath Nugget and he is left without anything, and yet the father is still saying to him that some things are best left unsaid, and it's impossible to shift the deadening, oppressive hand of keeping things secret.

> We are not speaking the truth about what has happened because
> of white guilt from having colluded in the oppression in the
> past.

This reflexive reading of the personal with the political is definitional of
Rayson's work. Louis Nowra has recently argued that while contemporary
English playwrights continue to be fascinated by class and the way it
determines experience, American playwrights are obsessed with the
self and the pursuit of happiness.[5] While Nowra also has some misgivings
about contemporary Australian theatre, however, it is clear that Rayson's
oeuvre represents a thorough-going commitment to the idea that theatre
should express politics as lived experience, and vice versa:

> [My plays] are entirely about bridging the public and the
> private, about trying to deal with private moments in the stories
> of people's lives set against the historical, social and political
> backdrop. Politics exists and is manifested in how we live.
> My task as a dramatist is to make the recognizable and the
> particular and the known shed light on the bigger canvas.
> People think about politics as being quite separate from the
> way they live their lives, and my entire raison d'être is to bring
> the two things together.

Inheritance achieves many things: it is an absorbing family saga full of
both affection and critique. And like many of Rayson's plays, here the
tragic and the comic are intermingled, one in dialogue with the other:
the wildly inappropriate dick jokes at a family funeral; Maureen and
Girlie's racist diatribe taking the piss out of every sacred cow; Felix's
well-intentioned 'Sorry' t-shirt, signalling his Brunswick Street cred,
while here in Rushton it epitomises everything laughable about urban
attitudes. The play revels in the ironic. Just as Dibs and Girlie settle the
question of inheritance, Lyle violently self-destructs. Maureen's political
rhetoric about helping the man on the land, turns out to be a matter of
political expedience when at the play's close she happily turfs them all
off the farm to finance her personal ambitions. Dramatic irony is a rich

---

[5] Louis Nowra, 'Just act normal', *Sydney Morning Herald*, 8 February 2003,
p.4.

vein running through this play, making audiences laugh in recognition, and then lose themselves in the profound emotional and moral turmoil at the heart of the work.

The irony also works to challenge whatever residual nostalgic and utopian ideas we might have about the country and the people who live there. As audiences, depending where we come from, we may view this play as a reworking of the iconic and romanticised view of the bush, a view that has come down to us through nineteenth-century art and literature, and then more recently reiterated in the period films of the Australian cinema in the 1970s and 1980s. There is much in *Inheritance* to suggest that the Australian countryside is not, and has never been, a place of great moral virtue, but a very dark place indeed—a place of terrible tragedies and repressions. And, as the play reminds us, this violence, inflicted on the self and on others, is historically patterned, each generation seeming doomed to repeat it. On the other hand, we might see this play as a critique of a political system which comprehensively abandoned the rural sector, turning country towns into nowhere-ville, and forcing their inhabitants to go without the most basic of services. Where this play is finally most remarkable is in its acknowledgement of a complex truth: alienation and despair provide the ideal preconditions for xenophobia. What a perfect scenario, this play shows us, for Hanson's politics of fear and blame.

This play is a hugely significant work of the Australian theatre; as significant in its own way as *Summer of the Seventeenth Doll*, or *The One Day of the Year* or *Don's Party*. Just as these canonical works once spoke to the hearts and minds of their respective generations, so does Rayson's play talk to us about who we are and what we believe. And this is no mean feat in an era when theatre seems increasingly to suffer from a certain timidity of spirit; less likely to take politics by the horns, and much more keen to take us into the psycho-sexual dramas of the middle class (a subject matter better handled by television in any case). In his history of British playwrighting, David Edgar argues that if the theatre is to thrive it needs to 'recapture its sense of the seriousness of its own mission. Faced with the fashionable contempt of those cultural critics who find theatre too much like hard work, theatre should celebrate rather than downplay the moral rigour of its endeavour, and return to its primary purpose of examining who we are and why we do what we do'.[6] Hannie Rayson's is an urgent, moral voice and it rings out in this play, reminding audiences that the theatre, at its best, is a place where dissent and contradiction lead to recognition and empathy—an antidote to the normalizing conservatism of our day.

Hilary Glow was the dramaturg on Inheritance *and has worked on Hannie Rayson's plays for more than a decade. She is currently based at the Australian Centre, University of Melbourne, where she is researching a PhD on contemporary Australian writing. The interview material with Rayson is taken from a forthcoming interview in* Meanjin.

---

[6] David Edgar (ed.) *State of Play*, Faber & Faber, London 1999, p.32.

Director's Note

Simon Phillips

Shortly after the triumphant premiere of her brilliant play *Life After George* at the MTC in 2000, we struck while the playwright was hot and asked Hannie what she wanted to write next for the company. She'd already decided: a huge family saga about the land. Such was the blindness of my faith in Hannie that I baulked not a jot at the idea of this essentially urban writer presenting to our essentially urban audience a view of the oft-romanticised or over-simplified Australian 'bush'.

One of the things I most admire in Hannie's approach to writing is her interest not only in enlightening us, but also in enlightening herself. Shying away from the personal experience or even personal opinion (although her heart shines through her work), she sets out to explore a topic about which *she* wants to know more. She has likened her approach to that of the investigative reporter, scraping away at every angle of a story, 'not in the name of balance or fairness, but in the quest for truth and complexity'. She has an instinct for the zeitgeist—but even there the word 'instinct' might offend her—her sense of the zeitgeist is borne of a passionate and intelligent focus on the world around her—no mere hunch but rather an informed reading of, and concern for, current affairs.

Thus, after probing the corporatisation of the tertiary education system in *Life After George*, she turned her attention to the farming community with two objectives: to collect first-hand what the central concerns of that community are in the twenty-first century, and to try to better understand the circumstances in which a figure like Pauline Hanson might have found a foothold in Australian politics.

Typically, she went on a rampage of research. Having accepted the commission she disappeared for two years, during which time she made regular visits to the Mallee, doing her investigative reporter thing and collecting stories, points of view, inhabiting the lives and minds of the people about whom she wished to write. She fell in and out of love with her subject matter as the warmer and uglier sides of their natures opened up to her apparently guileless and sympathetic probing.

The result of this approach to her writing is twofold. She tells the truth, or rather she tells truths, varied and opposing, but one finds them expressed in her plays, heartfelt and passionate, straight from the mouths of her characters. Whether Hannie herself likes the characters or not, they say it how they see it, without her censure. Thus any given person in the audience can find themselves cheering a different character on. Secondly, and this is a marvellous bi-product I think for a work of theatre, her characters' hearts beat and so we love them. Shakespeare wrote for an ensemble of actors and I often think that his characters have the benefit of his knowing the texture and detail of the real person who was going to play them. In Hannie's case, her characters are drawn together from threads of real people she has met (often the stories of several different people find themselves appropriated for one character's history or storyline), so they inherit the heartbeat of their genesis and as an audience it's hard not to view them with compassion, even if they horrify us.

Interestingly, this method of writing, which we affectionately refer to as the magpie approach, not only informs the development of the characters, but is ultimately reflected in the play's structure as well. The threads of the story are gathered together and at some point the spine of the plot is laid down (with a populist's eye for a damn good story), but because Hannie's concerns are both socio-political and humanist there are many aspects to the story which seem to float, waiting to find their emotional place in the nest. Hannie will hang on to an anecdote that has been lovingly passed on to her by someone, admitting that any form of rigour would see it turfed to the cutting room floor, but instead shuffling it through the story from one place to another, convinced that its presence will ultimately lend the story that extra layer of humanity.

In our early discussions about the play, Hannie surprised me by making comparison to a production I'd done of *The Seagull*. On the face of it, the structure of *Inheritance* is filmic, in the same way that Shakespeare is filmic, with often short scenes and sharp cuts from location to location. Chekhov tends to inhabit a single location, at least for an act at a time, letting his characters come and go. But her comment was a useful hint as to how she saw the play. Chekhov's plays bring together a community of people, thrust into each other's company by blood or circumstance, and the location seems to intensify their shortcomings and longings as their lives move inevitably forwards, usually towards seemingly inevitable disaster or despair. And that, essentially, is what Hannie has written here. In spite of the fact that the play never sticks literally in one location for more than a few pages, the overriding sense is of one location, a microcosmic family carrying the aspirations and desperations of an entire community, even a nation, inside its own personal story.

Melbourne
July 2003

To all the farmers, stockmen, shearers, stock-and-station agents, country publicans and exiles who told me their stories with such good humour and grace. Thank you.

Inheritance was first produced by Melbourne Theatre Company at the Playhouse, Victorian Arts Centre, on 5 March 2003, with the following cast:

DIBS HAMILTON	Monica Maughan
GIRLIE DELANEY	Lois Ramsey
FARLEY HAMILTON	Ronald Falk
WILLIAM HAMILTON	Rhys McConnochie
JULIA HAMILTON	Julie Nihill
FELIX HAMILTON-GRAY	Gareth Ellis
NUGGET HAMILTON	Wayne Blair
LYLE DELANEY	Steve Bisley
MAUREEN DELANEY	Geraldine Turner
ASHLEIGH DELANEY, YOUNG DIBS	Katherine Fyffe
BRIANNA DELANEY, YOUNG GIRLIE	Jody Kennedy
NORM MYRTLE, LUCKY JOE DELANEY	Nick Farnell

Director, Simon Phillips
Dramaturg, Hilary Glow
Set Designer, Shaun Gurton
Costume Designer, Tracy Grant
Lighting Designer, Nick Schlieper

CHARACTERS

T$_{HE}$ H$_{AMILTONS}$

DIBS HAMILTON, aged 80
FARLEY HAMILTON, aged 83, husband of Dibs
WILLIAM HAMILTON, aged 52, eldest son
JULIA HAMILTON, aged 44, daughter
FELIX HAMILTON-GRAY, aged 19, Julia's son
NUGGET HAMILTON, aged 38, adopted Aboriginal son

T$_{HE}$ D$_{ELANEYS}$

GIRLIE DELANEY, aged 80, Dibs' twin sister
LYLE DELANEY, aged 48, son of Girlie, farmer
MAUREEN DELANEY, aged 55, Lyle's wife
ASHLEIGH DELANEY, aged 16, daughter of Lyle and Maureen
BRIANNA DELANEY, aged 15, her sister

C$_{HARACTERS FROM THE PAST}$

NORM MYRTLE (1890-1934), father of Dibs and Girlie
YOUNG GIRLIE
YOUNG DIBS
WORMIE MCCALLUM (1915-1980), stockman
LUCKY JOE DELANEY (1920-1989), Girlie's husband
LOFTY BLAKE

PROLOGUE

Sunset in the Mallee. The sky is streaked with orange and red. Darkness is approaching. In the backyard of the Myrtle family farm, the water tank is in silhouette. There are rusty forty-four-gallon drums lying around. The yard is littered with old farm junk and various members of the Myrtle family, neighbours and friends. Birds are calling. Dogs bark.

It is December 1934.

As the audience take their seats, the actors gaze into the auditorium, quiet and impassive, as though watching strangers coming into town.

NORM MYRTLE *(the patriarch) plays the piano on the verandah.* WORMIE MCCALLUM *is accompanying him on the mouth organ.*

Suddenly night falls. A big spotlight, made from a roo spotter, falls on NORM. *He is holding a trophy made from a sheep's skull with a blue ribbon rosette.*

NORM: Ladies and gentlemen, a big, warm welcome to our first act of the evening. Competing for the 1934 Norm Myrtle Memorial Trophy, please put your hands together for our very own 'Darlings of the Mallee'—my two favourite girls—the Myrtle Twins.

> *The spotlight is directed at two towels hanging from a clothes line, making a circle of light.*

Dibs and Girlie Myrtle.

> NORM *strikes up the music. Two fourteen-year-old girls, dressed in blue, burst through 'the curtains' to sing 'Two Little Girls in Blue'. (Melody and text by Charles Graham, 1893.)*

DIBS & GIRLIE: [*together, singing*]
> An old man gazed on a photograph
> In a locket he'd worn for years;
> His nephew then asked him the reason why
> That picture had caused him tears.
> 'Come listen,' he said, 'I will tell you, lad,

A story that's strange, but true!
Your father and I, at the school one day,
Met two little girls in blue.

REFRAIN:

Two little girls in blue, lad,
Two little girls in blue.
They were sisters, we were brothers
And learned to love the two.
And one little girl in blue, lad,
Who won your father's heart,
Became your mother. I married the other,
Till destiny drew us apart.

But freedom and happiness filled our life,
A life that was fair and true—
For two better girls never lived than they,
Those two little girls in blue.'

The assembled crowd clap and whistle.

NORM: Ladies and gentlemen. The prima donnas of Allandale. Our very own queens of song, Dibs and Girlie Myrtle.

◆ ◆ ◆ ◆ ◆

ACT ONE

SCENE ONE

Midday in the Mallee. A country road.

There is an almighty explosion. A Toyota Corolla shudders to a halt. Smoke pours from the engine.

The driver is a woman in her forties, JULIA. *The passenger is her son,* FELIX. *They are clearly inner-city folk.*

JULIA: Fuck. [*Pause.*] Fuck fuck fuck fuck fuck.

> *They get out. As* JULIA *slams the door, the car explodes again. This time the bonnet springs open and water gushes out.*

Fuck.

> *Silence. They stare at the car.* FELIX *surveys the landscape. They are miles from anywhere. He goes to release the radiator cap and burns his hand.*

FELIX: Fuck!

JULIA: Felix!

> *He kicks the tyre. A black crow comments: Faarrk, faarrk!*
>
> *He leans against the car.*

FELIX: Where are we?

JULIA: On the Berriwillock Road.

FELIX: And how far is Rushton? Approximately.

JULIA: About forty ks.

FELIX: Too far to walk. Obviously.

> JULIA *examines things under the bonnet.* FELIX *leans on the roof of the car and squints into the distance.*

JULIA: Black smoke means a fuel system defect.

FELIX: [*to the audience*] I hate cars.

JULIA: Blue smoke means internal engine problems.

FELIX: [*to the audience*] I don't even have a licence.

JULIA: And white smoke is the result of coolant getting into the cylinders.

FELIX: [*to the audience*] My mother did a course in Car Maintenance For Women. So we should be back on the road in no time. I'm Felix. I live above the Cosmic Kebab in Sydney Road.

JULIA: I think it's the head gasket.

FELIX: That did occur to me, but I didn't want to be alarmist.

JULIA: Felix, can you pass me a spanner? From the boot.

FELIX: Spanner… spanner…

He hands her a screwdriver.

Spanner.

JULIA: That's a screwdriver.

FELIX: Right.

He dives back into the car and hands her a spanner. She holds up the two tools.

JULIA: Spanner. Screwdriver.

She returns to the business under the bonnet.

FELIX: [*to the audience*] This is my mother, Julia.

JULIA: [*to the audience*] Hi.

FELIX: [*to the audience*] She always takes on this passive-aggressive tone when she wants me to come up to Allandale with her.

JULIA: What are you talking about?

FELIX [*mimicking*] It's just that it's your nanna's eightieth birthday and everyone would be so sad if you weren't there.

JULIA: You didn't have to come.

FELIX: [*mimicking*] But we'd all be very disappointed if you didn't.

❖ ❖ ❖ ❖ ❖

SCENE TWO

The Hamiltons' farm.

DIBS *walks across the stage with a wheelbarrow of dirt. Her twin sister* GIRLIE *enters.*

DIBS: [*to the audience*] We were all very disappointed when Julia and Hamish separated. I'm Dibs. Julia's mother. She's coming up this weekend, for our birthday. Girlie's and mine. We're eighty tomorrow.

> *She tips the dirt out.*

GIRLIE: [*to the audience*] Old as God's dog. [*To* DIBS] I hope you're not using blood and bone on those roses.

DIBS: No.

GIRLIE: [*to the audience*] She is, you know. She'll burn the roots. [*To* DIBS] You'll burn the roots.

DIBS: Righto.

> DIBS *spades the dirt onto the roses.*

GIRLIE: [*to the audience*] See! Doesn't take a jot of notice. [*To* DIBS] D'you see where Kyneton Boy came home in the third at Cranbourne.

DIBS: D'you have any money on it?

GIRLIE: I gave that silly son o' mine, ten quid. D'you think he remembered to go to the TAB?

DIBS: He's got a lot on his plate, poor ol' Lyle.

GIRLIE: Poor ol' Lyle, my arse. Came in at seven-to-one.

DIBS: Jeepers.

GIRLIE: Always had the luck of a speckle-arsed rooster. [*She grabs her coat.*] Well, I'm off home.

DIBS: Righto.

> GIRLIE *exits.*

[*To the audience*] It's a terrible thing when a marriage ends. Mind you, I don't think Julia tried hard enough. That's the thing with young women: too selfish by half. I thought he was lovely—Hamish. I miss him. He came up one Easter and helped me plant the lavender hedge, over there. Sometimes in the spring when I come out for herbs and I see the lavender in full bloom, I say, 'Hello Hamish'.

◆ ◆ ◆ ◆ ◆

SCENE THREE

The Delaneys'.

A little run-down house on the outskirts of Rushton. GIRLIE *lives there with* LYLE *and his family. There are car bodies in the yard and a rusty, swinging seat with plastic cushions on the verandah.*

LYLE *comes looking for his mother. On the front path there is a large object with a blanket over it.*

LYLE: You there, Girlie? Mum? You there?
GIRLIE: [*offstage*] Only just.

> GIRLIE *enters.*

What's this?
LYLE: Happy birthday.
GIRLIE: What is it, Lyle?
LYLE: Na-nah!

> *He unveils the object. It is a motorised lawn-mower that he has converted into a little drive-bike for his mother. Long pause.* GIRLIE *stares at it.*

GIRLIE: Do I have to do m' own lawns now?
LYLE: Come on. Hop on.
GIRLIE: Don't be ridiculous.
LYLE: This is going to make all the difference to your life, Mum.
GIRLIE: Too right it is. I'm gonna be the town idiot.
LYLE: Look. Pull the cord. And away you go.

> *He demonstrates.*

GIRLIE: You expect me to ride down the main street of Rushton on a
   dead man's lawn-mower. Anyway, it's clapped out.

LYLE: It's not clapped out. It's beautiful. I reconditioned the motor. C'mon, give it a go. [*Pause.*] Don't be a piker.

GIRLIE: Jesus Christ.

LYLE: That's the spirit.

> *She clambers on, refusing his assistance.* LYLE *pulls the starter-cord and the machine roars to life.*

Put your foot on the pedal!

GIRLIE: Jesus H. Christ!

> *The bike leaps into action, carrying* GIRLIE *offstage.*

◆ ◆ ◆ ◆ ◆

SCENE FOUR

In the Hamiltons' farmhouse kitchen, DIBS *is arranging some roses in a vase.* WILLIAM *comes up the path. He is carrying bags. Dogs bark excitedly.*

DIBS: Will! I didn't hear the car.

WILLIAM: Deaf as well as everything else.

> *They embrace.*

Happy birthday.

DIBS: [*to the dogs*] Settle down, Blackie! [*To* WILLIAM] Thanks, darling. [*To the dogs*] Mack! Shut up! [*To* WILLIAM] Julia's broken down on the Berriwillock Road.

WILLIAM: Not again.

DIBS: I thought you might have passed her.

WILLIAM: No. I never come that way.

DIBS: You turn off at Wycheproof, do you?

WILLIAM: Yeah. Up through Quambatook. Why does she persist with that old bomb?

DIBS: She likes old things.

WILLIAM: Handy for you.

◆ ◆ ◆ ◆ ◆

SCENE FIVE

On the Berriwillock Road.

JULIA *and* FELIX *wait by the side of the road with their car.*

FELIX: How long before we die of thirst, do you reckon?

JULIA: We may have to drink our own urine.

FELIX: You are a very strange woman.

JULIA: If you follow that line of trees over there, that's the southern fence of Maloneys'. I went to school with Donger Maloney.

FELIX: Oh, purlease.

JULIA: We had a level of sophistication of which you could only dream. Donger won first prize in the faggot races one New Year's Eve.

FELIX: Faggot races?

JULIA: Yeah, you get a few blokes. Five or six. And they all line up outside the pub. Stark naked. And each one clenches a rolled-up newspaper in their bum. They sort of hold it between the cheeks. Then a bloke behind them lights the newspaper and Waxy Kirk yells 'Go' and they sort of shuffle down to the river and jump in before their arses catch fire.

FELIX: Right.

JULIA: It's pretty funny.

She is very amused by the memory.

FELIX: Uh-huh.

◆ ◆ ◆ ◆ ◆

SCENE SIX

GIRLIE *hoons across the stage sitting atop her new motor.*

GIRLIE: Crikey O'Reilly, where's the brakes?

LYLE: On the side. On the side!

She lurches to a halt.

What d'you reckon?

  Pause.

GIRLIE: You're a bloody menace.

LYLE: I had a call from Val Barker, by the way. They're all coming.

GIRLIE: From Chinkapook? Oh, gawd. How many's that, now?

LYLE: 'Bout sixty.

GIRLIE: We're gonna need more grog.

LYLE: Keep your hair on.

GIRLIE: You don't know those Barkers. They drink like fish. [*Pause.*]
    What do they want, coming to our birthday?

LYLE: Must be someone asked 'em.

◆ ◆ ◆ ◆ ◆

SCENE SEVEN

The Hamiltons' kitchen.

DIBS *is making sandwiches.*

DIBS: I asked the Barkers, by the way.

GIRLIE: [*to* LYLE] Don't just stand there. Power me up!

WILLIAM: Not Emu Barker? He stoushed me in primary school.

DIBS: That was forty years ago, love.

WILLIAM: You don't think he'll try it again, do you?

  LYLE *pulls the cord.* GIRLIE *roars off.*

DIBS: I saw Mrs Barker at the CWA—she's on with Cougar Cogsley.
    Did I tell you?

WILLIAM: Who's Cougar Cogsley?

DIBS: He's a financial counsellor. In Rotary with Dad. He's a bit boring
    actually.

WILLIAM: Boring? Gosh. I'm surprised they let him into Rotary.

DIBS: You didn't bring Kevin?

WILLIAM: He'd rather stick pins in his eyes.

DIBS: He'd be very welcome, any time.

WILLIAM: He would not. Gay men are not welcome in Rushton. Trust me on this.

DIBS: Well, nobody need know. He doesn't have to advertise the fact.

> WILLIAM *shakes his head. A mousetrap snaps shut.* DIBS *moves to collect it.*

Don't forget to tuck your eiderdown in tight. We're having a bit of trouble with mice.

WILLIAM: Not again.

DIBS: Dad found one in the toaster this morning.

> *A feisty weather-beaten old man enters,* FARLEY.

FARLEY: Here's trouble.

WILLIAM: [*to the audience*] Speaking of *Der Führer*. [*To* FARLEY] Father. How are you?

FARLEY: Nothing a bit of rain wouldn't fix.

DIBS: [*going to the door to dispose of the mouse*] We had an inch last week.

WILLIAM: Really?

FARLEY: [*helping himself to a sandwich*] Worse than '82 now, much worse. When did you get here?

WILLIAM: Just arrived.

FARLEY: Good. You can give me a hand down at Burns's.

DIBS: He's just got in, love.

FARLEY: What have you done with the air compressor?

WILLIAM: I've just got here. From the city.

DIBS: [*going to the phone*] Julia's broken down on the Berriwillock Road.

FARLEY: Last rain, blimey near thirty-five points we got, didn't we?

WILLIAM: That was a couple of years ago now, Dad.

FARLEY: Green barley shoots all through the stubble. Bloody beautiful. I don't know how you can live down there. I said to Mum… what did I say?

DIBS: You said you wouldn't like to live in the city.

FARLEY: That's right.

DIBS: [*into the phone*] Come on, Nugget. Pick up.

FARLEY: Two weeks and you'd have a suicide on your hands.

WILLIAM: How very operatic of you, Father.

DIBS: [*hanging up*] Nugget's not answering his phone.

WILLIAM: I'll go, Mum.

DIBS: No, don't be silly.

FARLEY: I'm not planning on leaving this place. I'll tell you that for nothing. They'll be carting me outta here with me boots on, when the time comes.

> FARLEY *exits. The flywire screen slaps shut.*

[*Offstage, to the dogs*] Eh! Blackie! Git outta there! Go'on! Git! You flea-bitten mongrel!

WILLIAM: Hello, William. How are you? Are you well? How nice of you to come all this way to see us.

DIBS: [*dialling again*] At least he remembered you.

WILLIAM: Instead of 'Hey you, you little sissy!'

DIBS: Let's not go down that track.

WILLIAM: No. Let's pretend that he has the capacity to treat his son slightly better than his dogs.

DIBS: [*into the phone*] Nuggs! Mum here. Where are you?

◆ ◆ ◆ ◆ ◆

SCENE EIGHT

In the paddock.

NUGGET *is talking on his mobile.*

NUGGET: [*into the phone*] Down at Cromies'. Giving Lyle a hand.

LYLE: Hey, Nugget?

> NUGGET *lifts a hand to silence* LYLE.

DIBS: [*into the phone*] Julia's broken down on the Berriwillock Road.

NUGGET: [*into the phone*] Not again. Okay. Give me ten minutes.

LYLE: What's up?

NUGGET: I'm off, mate. Got to get Jules. Corolla's shat itself again.

LYLE: Listen, mate. 'Bout that seeder Jack Cummins has got for sale?

NUGGET: I've already said: we're better off using a contractor.

LYLE: Mate. I want to be me own boss—not hanging around waiting for Floppy Fuckin' Mitchell to show up.

NUGGET: And I'm not having a hundred-grand worth of machinery rusting in the shed for eleven months of the year.

LYLE: Look. We go halves.

NUGGET: No.

LYLE: Fifty grand each.

NUGGET: No, mate.

LYLE: It's a bloody good buy, Nugget. You're bein' a mug.

NUGGET: Wouldn't be the first time.

> NUGGET *exits.*

LYLE: You can't wait for things to come to you, you know. You've got to make things happen.

◆ ◆ ◆ ◆ ◆

SCENE NINE

On the Berriwillock Road.

FELIX: You sort of wait, don't you? Wait for something to happen.

JULIA: Your generation is just soft.

FELIX: Excuse me?

JULIA: You want your experiences in the safety of the retail zone.

FELIX: Yeah, right.

JULIA: You want ersatz adventure from playing games on the computer or taking drugs.

FELIX: And like this is where it's really happening.

> *Pause.*

JULIA: I need to talk to you about something.

FELIX: I hate it when you kick off like that.

JULIA: One of the reasons I wanted you to come up to Allandale—

FELIX: [*dubiously*] Yes?

JULIA: I suppose this is as good a time as any—

FELIX: Since we are suspended in the limbo between Being and Nothingness.

JULIA: I'm pretty sure, well I am. I'm certain. I'm pregnant.

FELIX: Oh, shit.

JULIA: Ten weeks pregnant.

FELIX: Mum, you're forty-three.

JULIA: Forty-four.

FELIX: Isn't that a bit old?

JULIA: Apparently not.

FELIX: You're certain about this?

JULIA: Yes.

FELIX: And you're actually thinking... no, you're not. Sorry. [*Neutral*] So, are you planning to go ahead with this pregnancy?

JULIA: Yes.

FELIX: And do you mind if I ask—?

JULIA: Graham. From work.

FELIX: That short Indian bloke?

JULIA: No, that's Amitav. [*Pause.*] Graham's the tall Indian bloke.

FELIX: You're planning to tell them about this. Nanna Dibs and Grandpa.

JULIA: Mm-hmm.

FELIX: This weekend?

JULIA: They have to know, sooner or later.

FELIX: Are you going to tell them that it'll be a little brown baby?

◆ ◆ ◆ ◆ ◆

SCENE TEN

GIRLIE *and* MAUREEN *walk down the main street of Rushton.* GIRLIE *is on her frame,* MAUREEN *assisting.*

GIRLIE: You'll never guess what she's done now.

MAUREEN: Who?

GIRLIE: Dibs. She's gone and asked the wogs.

Lois Ramsey as Girlie in the 2003 Melbourne Theatre Company production. (Photo: Jeff Busby)

MAUREEN: The Pappases? From the pub? Christ.

GIRLIE: Honest to God. [*To the audience*] I said to Maureen—this is my daughter-in-law, Maureen.

MAUREEN: [*to the audience*] G'day.

GIRLIE: [*to the audience*] I said to Maureen, she's asking people willy-nilly and it's not as if she'll get more food in. We're looking after the grog—our side—but I don't know what she thinks we're all gonna eat. My sister is a very Christian woman—Dibs—but when it comes down to it—she's as mean as all get-out. It's the Presbyterian in her. Stingy. Here, cross the road. I don't like walking past the pub.

MAUREEN: They know it was you dobbed them in, you know.

GIRLIE: Serves them right. [*Yelling*] Pack o' cheats!

MAUREEN: Sshh.

GIRLIE: You can't water down your vodka and expect to get away with it.

MAUREEN: If it's true.

GIRLIE: It's true. Fifteen dollars for a plate of steak and chips. Daylight robbery. There's people in this town can't afford a raffle ticket.

MAUREEN: People gotta eat.

GIRLIE: When we ran the place—never charged anything over a tenna. [*Yelling*] They're thieves, those Greeks!

MAUREEN: Girlie!

GIRLIE: Blow-ins. And they don't pay tax neither. Who do they think pays for the roads and the schools and that?

MAUREEN: Their boy put in a good game in the ruck last Saturday.

GIRLIE: Still a wog.

MAUREEN: I hear young Felix has got himself a new girlfriend. [*Pause.*] Japanese.

GIRLIE: Oh, Christ All-Bloody-Mighty.

MAUREEN: I thought he was a homo.

GIRLIE: I dunno why the mother doesn't put her foot down.

MAUREEN: Julia?! She probably put him up to it. She's a big shot in the whole multicultural racket. That's her job down there.

GIRLIE: What about I order a couple dozen sausage rolls?

MAUREEN: Yeah. Maybe some party pies.

GIRLIE: Some quiche lorraines, too, I reckon.

MAUREEN: Are they the ones with bacon in them?

GIRLIE: So what?

MAUREEN: We need something for the vegetarians.

GIRLIE: Bugger the vegetarians.

◆ ◆ ◆ ◆ ◆

SCENE ELEVEN

The Hamiltons'.

DIBS *and* WILLIAM *are carrying in more boxes for the party. Dogs bark.*

WILLIAM: I've made an appointment with the social worker for next week.

DIBS: I think we might just muddle on, love.

WILLIAM: He's going to need full-time care. Pretty soon.

DIBS: We're doing all right. In our own way.

WILLIAM: Mum, the waiting list is three years.

> *Silence.*

Mum?

DIBS: He's really not that bad. Most days.

WILLIAM: Oh, come on.

DIBS: Some days he's perfectly lucid.

WILLIAM: He is deteriorating rapidly.

DIBS: You don't understand how truly awful it would be for him to leave the farm.

WILLIAM: The important thing now is not to be too influenced by what he's feeling. Because he's very addled and soon he will be completely gone. What matters now is you. Okay? Have you told Julia yet?

DIBS: Told Julia what?

WILLIAM: That we're selling the farm.

DIBS: No…

> *Silence.*

WILLIAM: [*quietly*] I thought this was the whole purpose of having the party. So you could tell everybody.

DIBS: I haven't even had a chance to discuss it with Girlie yet.

WILLIAM: It's none of her business. Look. You've been whingeing about this house all our lives. Stick to your guns and you will have your own brand new home.

DIBS: I know.

WILLIAM: With a view of the sea—on the Mornington Peninsula. No dust storms. No mouse shit. No possums pissing in the roof.

DIBS: No friends.

WILLIAM: I thought you wanted to be near us.

DIBS: I do.

WILLIAM: Near town, but not 'boxed in'.

DIBS: But what's Nugget going to do?

WILLIAM: Oh, for heaven's sake. Nugget is a grown man.

DIBS: If I sell this place, Nugget will be a farmer without a farm.

WILLIAM: We've been over this, Mum. There's a job there for Nugget if he wants it.

DIBS: He doesn't know anything about grapes. And neither do you, for that matter.

WILLIAM: As I've said—Kevin will be running the vineyard and I will be running the restaurant.

DIBS: And what will Nugget be running?

> NUGGET *enters.*

NUGGET: What am I running?

WILLIAM: Hey. Mate. Nugget! How are you?

NUGGET: Saw your car out front.

WILLIAM: Yeah. I was just askin' how you're getting on. Sounds like pretty good. What you been up to?

NUGGET: Over at Lyle's place. Helping him with his bloody lambs.

> NUGGET *drinks milk from the carton.*

DIBS: You're a good stick, Nuggs. Glass.

NUGGET: His mulesing bloke didn't show.

DIBS: Shorty Farrell. He's a hopeless case, isn't he?

WILLIAM: You've been mulesing, have you?

NUGGET: Tail-docking. Jeez, I hate sheep.

DIBS: Lyle loves them, doesn't he?

NUGGET: He needs his head read. So what am I running?

WILLIAM: A raffle, mate.

NUGGET: Uh-huh. [*Pause.*] Where are m' keys? Better rescue Jules, eh?

WILLIAM: I'll go if you like.

NUGGET: You can help Waxy knock in a few fence posts.

WILLIAM: No thanks.

NUGGET: It's called farming, mate.

> DIBS *throws the keys.* NUGGET *catches them.*

See yous in the soup.

◆ ◆ ◆ ◆ ◆

SCENE TWELVE

The Delaneys'.

GIRLIE *is wiping down the table.* MAUREEN *is making lunch.* BRIANNA *is on the verandah, unpacking some paint from a box.* ASHLEIGH *enters with a suitcase.*

ASHLEIGH: Nan? When you die—

MAUREEN: Ashleigh!

ASHLEIGH: We're all gonna die, Mum.

GIRLIE: Just some sooner than others. What, darl?

ASHLEIGH: Can I have this?

> GIRLIE *looks in the old suitcase.*

GIRLIE: I haven't seen this for years. Look. Little shoes and a curl, from my baby brother Donald. He died of scarlet fever when he was three. Dibs knitted him this little red cap [*holding it up*] so we could always see where he was in the wheat.

MAUREEN: Oh, isn't that sweet? Bri, come and fix the sandwiches please.

BRIANNA: Awww?

MAUREEN: Ashleigh did the chooks. Come on, Bri, please.

ASHLEIGH: Hey, Bri. Pigeon tags. Look.

> BRIANNA *joins* ASHLEIGH *and* GIRLIE *at the suitcase.*

GIRLIE: Our mother would line this suitcase with a couple of tea towels and pack it with cream horns—they were her thing—ginger fluffs, asparagus rolls, lamingtons, cheese boats.

MAUREEN: Jeez, that'd stack it on.

> *Meanwhile* ASHLEIGH *has taken a package out of the suitcase. She puts on a man-sized Father Christmas hat and beard.*

ASHLEIGH: Ho! Ho! Ho!

GIRLIE: Take that off.

ASHLEIGH: Merry Christmas!

GIRLIE: For chrissake. Take it off!

> *She grabs it off her.*

ASHLEIGH: Ohhhh.

GIRLIE: Just do as I say. You stupid girl. For once in your life.

> GIRLIE *stuffs the hat and beard in the suitcase, snaps it closed and exits.*

◆ ◆ ◆ ◆ ◆

SCENE THIRTEEN

Berriwillock Road.

We hear the tooting of a ute in the distance, whirring up dust as it barrels along a dirt road.

JULIA: That looks like Nugget.

FELIX: I still can't believe we call him *Nugget.*

JULIA: That's his name.

FELIX: His name's Neville.

JULIA: Yeah, well he's never been called Neville in his life.

FELIX: It's like calling him *Coon.*

JULIA: It is not.

FELIX: It is. It's off.

Silence. NUGGET *pulls up and ambles over.*

JULIA: Nugget. G'day.

They hug.

NUGGET: How are ya, Sis? Jeez, I would'na reconnised you. You've stacked it on, since Easter.

JULIA: Thanks.

JULIA *and* FELIX *exchange glances.*

NUGGET: Let me look at you.

FELIX: Got a way with women, these country blokes.

NUGGET: [*to* FELIX] How are you, mate? Still a real asphalt fella. Eh?

FELIX: How can you tell?

NUGGET: The shoes, mate.

FELIX: At least I know which way to catch the tram into town.

NUGGET: [*to the audience*] Four hours it took me to get from Carlton to the city.

FELIX: He went via La Trobe University.

NUGGET: Bloody nightmare. [*Pause. To* JULIA] You're lookin' good, Sis. Divorce agrees with ya.

JULIA: Sorry about Annie.

NUGGET: Yeah. Cleared out about a month ago. It was hard for her, you know.

JULIA: What? Living out here?

NUGGET: They can make it pretty rough. White teacher living with a blackfella. Even the kids in her class were having a go at her.

FELIX: That's such crap.

JULIA: Oh, Nuggs. I'm so sorry.

NUGGET: I lost me girl, you lost your bloke. What's the matter with us, Jules?

JULIA: I don't know.

FELIX: William's still with Kevin.

NUGGET: Yeah, well.

JULIA: Kevin is lovely.

NUGGET: I just don't like to think about it.

JULIA: You are incorrigible.

NUGGET: [*to* FELIX] Come on, give us a hand. [*Indicating the shoes*] Can you walk in those things?

FELIX: I'm very comfortable. Thank you for enquiring.

NUGGET: [*to* FELIX] Grab the rope, will you? It's in the tray.

> FELIX *exits. Pause.*

[*To* JULIA] You don't think the old girl's gonna leave me high and dry, do you, Jules?

JULIA: What do you mean?

NUGGET: Sell up from under me?

JULIA: Why would she do that?

NUGGET: She's been goin' up to town a lot to see that financial counsellor bloke.

JULIA: Maybe she's having an affair.

NUGGET: Yeah, sure.

JULIA: Hey, she's eighty years old. She's not going to sell up and move on now.

NUGGET: Brother William's been in her ear.

JULIA: What?

NUGGET: He's been up here three weekends in a row.

JULIA: He didn't tell me that. Maybe he's worried about Dad. He thinks he should be in care.

NUGGET: Yeah, well that's bullshit. Farley's not doing anyone any harm.

> FELIX *approaches with the rope.*

[*To* FELIX] Good on you, mate. [*To* JULIA] They'd be up shit creek, you know, if it wasn't for me.

JULIA: Running the farm?

NUGGET: It was me talked 'em into getting rid of the sheep.

JULIA: Mum said.

NUGGET: Just because Lyle's re-stocking on his place. See Lyle and me, we don't see eye-to-eye on this. It's bloody crazy. He's throwing away ten grand a paddock.

JULIA: That's what you'd make on wheat, is it?

NUGGET: Bloody oath. You're just wasting your paddock, grazing sheep on this country.

FELIX: But you must make something on sheep?

NUGGET: Not that kind of dough. Not anymore. Not by the time you build in all your labour costs and your extra travelling and everything else. It's best for us to specialise as grain growers and do a damn good job—rather than run two enterprises. [*To* FELIX] Tow bar.

He hands the knotted rope to FELIX, *who exits.*

JULIA: What does Dad say?

NUGGET: He's had a gutful of Lyle. See, me and Farley, we've always had an understanding.

JULIA: How d'you mean?

NUGGET: About the farm.

JULIA: What about the farm?

NUGGET: When the time comes—it's no good carving it up. That's no good for anyone. I'm just worried that other people are gonna muscle in. Just because Farley's not a hundred percent up top—doesn't mean you can sell his farm from under him.

◆ ◆ ◆ ◆ ◆

SCENE FOURTEEN

The Hamiltons' kitchen.

FARLEY *is standing on a chair as* DIBS *pins up his trousers.* FARLEY *is restless.* DIBS *has pins in her mouth.*

FARLEY: This won't buy the baby a dress.

DIBS: Just a minute.

FARLEY: Some of us have got work to do.

DIBS: Hold your horses. [*To* WILLIAM] I got these [*trousers*] at Kirbys' garage sale. Fifteen dollars.

WILLIAM: Dead man's trousers?

DIBS: I don't reckon they've ever been worn.

FARLEY: She wanted me to get new ones. New trousers for one night. Bloody ridiculous.

WILLIAM: That's what people do, you know. When there's a special occasion. They buy themselves some new clothes.

FARLEY: Is that so? Aren't I a fool?

DIBS: Okay. Hop down.

WILLIAM: It's not as if you can't afford it.

FARLEY: No, I'm just a miserable old skinflint.

DIBS: Okay. All done.

WILLIAM: It's not like you've spent your whole life throwing parties.

DIBS: Hop down, Farl.

FARLEY: Oh, what a fool am I. Good lord. I can see that now. To think that all these years I've been scrimping so I could send my children to Scotch College. When I could have been poncing about—

DIBS: Pop into the bedroom, love.

FARLEY: How the scales have fallen. What a buffoon. What an imbecile.

DIBS: Put your old trousers back on.

FARLEY: Frittering away all that money. On education. Good God. The waste. As if we ever saw any results. Ha! As if you ever showed yourself to be anything—

DIBS: Into the bedroom.

FARLEY: Anything. Anything at all but a—

WILLIAM: But a—what?

   Silence.

FARLEY: Obviously there are people in this world who can't overcome their own… weakness.

DIBS: Off you go now.

   FARLEY *exits, ushered out by* DIBS.

WILLIAM: [*to the audience*] I remember going with him to the Show. The Rushton A & P. [*Agricultural and Pastoral*] It was the only exciting thing that ever happened in this shit-heap. Every November—down by the river. The whole area was covered with fairy lights and tents and showground music. There was Sharman's

Boxing Troupe and Big Chief Little Wolf, the Globe of Death, the half-man half-lady and Vanessa the Undresser.

But the thing I wanted. The thing I'd saved for all year, was this little jumping spider. I was about eight, I suppose. Anyway, this spider had a tube attached to a little pump and when you squeezed it, it made the spider jump. So I put my two-and-six on the counter. And I said to the bloke, 'A jumping spider please'. And as he pushed it toward me, my father swiped the money off the counter and he said, 'If you're going to waste my hard-earned money on rubbish, I'll take it back'. And he pocketed the two-and-six and walked off.

◆ ◆ ◆ ◆ ◆

SCENE FIFTEEN

The Delaneys'.

LYLE *is leafing through a brochure for farm machinery.*

MAUREEN: Stop drooling. You're not in the market for new machinery.
LYLE: Get off m' back, Maureen. [*To* GIRLIE] I'm going to see Jack
    Cummins about that three-tonne seeder.
GIRLIE: He selling, is he?
MAUREEN: Lyle!
LYLE: What?
MAUREEN: We can't even afford to let the girls go to the pictures.
LYLE: I'd shut up if I were you.

> *He swipes a bill off the table where* MAUREEN *has been working on the books.*

I'll pay this. What is it? [*He looks.*] Gas.

> MAUREEN *grabs it off him.*

MAUREEN: Forget it. There's not enough money in the cheque book.
LYLE: Just watch it, you.
MAUREEN: I'm the one keeping this family together. I'm the one who
    treks off to Swan Hill every bloody day to work in that shop.
LYLE: So you keep telling us.

MAUREEN: I'm putting in a sixty-hour week—for what? We're going down the toilet and you won't do a damn thing about it.

GIRLIE: It's not Lyle's fault.

MAUREEN: Why not?

GIRLIE: Because he's working himself into the ground and not making much money.

MAUREEN: No money, you mean.

GIRLIE: You can't help yourself, can you?

MAUREEN: Because he won't face facts. He can't make that farm pay.

GIRLIE: Lyle's a good farmer.

MAUREEN: He is a share farmer. We are paying one third of every dollar we earn to your sister and her miserable demented husband.

GIRLIE: You never know what's around the corner.

MAUREEN: Oh, yes. If we just keep hanging on, we'll get Allandale!

GIRLIE: You don't know what the future's got in store. You just have to take it day by day.

MAUREEN: It's bloody feudal. We're living like peasants.

LYLE: Nobody's forcing you to stick around.

> MAUREEN *notices* BRIANNA *is at the kitchen door.*

MAUREEN: What is it, Brianna?

BRIANNA: I think some of the pigeons are sick.

MAUREEN: Put them in a sack and drown them in the river. We can't afford to keep pigeons.

> LYLE *pushes past her and exits.*

❖ ❖ ❖ ❖ ❖

SCENE SIXTEEN

The Hamiltons'.

WILLIAM *has his sleeves rolled up and is preparing food on the kitchen table.* DIBS *enters.*

DIBS: What's this?

WILLIAM: Chicken wings with soy sauce and sesame seeds.

DIBS: Oh, my godfather!

WILLIAM: You can't feed sixty people with a plate of sandwiches, Mother.

DIBS: I know. [*Surveying the table*] What are these?

WILLIAM: Asparagus and prosciutto parcels. And these are little zucchini and goat's cheese pizzas.

DIBS: Good heavens.

WILLIAM: I trust that zucchini have made an appearance in the Mallee, since I was a child?

DIBS: At the CFA lunch the other day—Nelly Billcott made her own fokaishas [*focaccias*]. So there, smarty farty.

WILLIAM: Made her own what?

DIBS: Fokaishas. See! We're up with it.

> WILLIAM *suppresses a grin.*

WILLIAM: What about cream horns? We having them?

DIBS: Cream horns. They were your Grandpa Norm's favourite.

> DIBS *remembers her dad:*

> GRANDPA NORM *enters with* YOUNG DIBS.

NORM: How 'bout some o' those cream horns your mum fixed? They're my favourite.

YOUNG DIBS: Want a cup of tea?

NORM: That'd be grand, Princess. I'm that dry, I could drink from a Chinaman's boot.

DIBS: Poor Dad. It was all too hard, trying to scratch a living. He was getting one-and-six a bushel. And then on top of that—running the farm—he was doing every dead-end job he could get. Trapping rabbits. Chopping wood. Filling in at the butchers.

NORM: I was closin' up the butcher shop this morning. Only had a coupla minutes before the footy bus, when Mrs Barker comes in and she says, 'I want a chook, Norm. I've got some unexpected visitors.' Any rate, I've only got one chicken left. 'Two-and-six', I said. 'Ooh, it looks a bit small. See if you've got something bigger.' So I ran out the back, put the chicken on the block and I smacked him a coupla times with the flat of the meat cleaver. I stretched his neck, pulled his wings out and put me fist inside the carcass and punched him out a bit, and then I ran out and said, 'How's that for size Mrs Barker?' And she says, 'How much is that one, Norm?' And I said, 'Four-and-six'. She said, 'Good, I'll take it. And you may as well wrap up the other one too.'

NORM *exits, chuckling.*

DIBS *snaps out of her memory.*

DIBS: Something must have just snapped, you know, Will.

WILLIAM: What?

DIBS: Dad. Don't know what it was. He'd be laughing away, life of the party, and then he'd get a visit from the black dog.

WILLIAM: Yeah.

DIBS: You know who he reminds me of? Lyle Delaney.

◆ ◆ ◆ ◆ ◆

SCENE SEVENTEEN

LYLE *and* BRIANNA *are on bicycles, laughing as they hare along a track on the farm. They come to a stop in a paddock a long way from the house. They have pigeons in baskets on the handlebars.*

LYLE: [*laughing and out of breath*] How about here? This looks like a good spot.

BRIANNA: Can I do the first toss?

LYLE: Can't see why not.

BRIANNA: What happens if they don't make it back to the house?

LYLE: Well. We've put in all the work. Training them up. As long as there aren't too many hawks up there, they'll fly straight home. You put in the work and you get your rewards. But you gotta have a bit of faith too.

BRIANNA *takes out a pigeon and tosses it in the air. And then another.*

BRIANNA: There they go! Fly home, pigeons. Fly home!

She jumps on her bike happily and pelts back the way they came.

[*As she goes*] Carn, Dad!

LYLE: Hang on.

> *He takes his pigeon out carefully and kisses her on the head.*

Here you are, Princess.

> *He watches* BRIANNA *riding furiously as he talks to his bird, cupped in his big hands.*

You beautiful girl. Make the most of it up there.

BRIANNA: [*calling*] Dad! Hurry up.

LYLE: Coming! [*To the pigeon*] Don't let me down, girl.

> *He tosses his pigeon and jumps on his bike.*

[*Calling as he goes off*] Last one home's a rotten egg!

◆ ◆ ◆ ◆ ◆

SCENE EIGHTEEN

The Delaneys'.

MAUREEN *is in the kitchen.* GIRLIE *passes through with her suitcase.* ASHLEIGH *enters wearing a very short skirt. She is humming a hymn in preparation for choir.*

MAUREEN: Ashleigh, love, I don't think so.

ASHLEIGH: What?

MAUREEN: The skirt, darl. No way.

ASHLEIGH: What's the matter with it?

MAUREEN: You're not leaving anything to the imagination there.

ASHLEIGH: So?

MAUREEN: Sweetheart. You need to create a bit of mystery. Isn't that right, Girl?

GIRLIE: Oh, yeah.

ASHLEIGH: I don't have another skirt.

MAUREEN: What about that nice navy one?

ASHLEIGH: The zip's busted. And I hate that skirt. I look like a Salvo.

MAUREEN: What say we go in to Swan Hill and see what we can find, eh?

ASHLEIGH: I'd rather go to Melbourne.

MAUREEN: We'll see.

ASHLEIGH: When? Mum? When?

GIRLIE: [*to the audience*] Never's too soon. If you ask me. It's bad luck, that place. Dibs used to like it. When she was nursing. She and Dulcie—Dulcie Shaw—they used to go to the Australia Hotel on Friday nights and have gin slings. I was doing a secretarial course at Stott's. One time the three of us went to the Embassy nightclub. They had a big orchestra and the conductor was all done up in a blue tuxedo which matched his eyes. Dibs thought he was a bit of all right. She was wearing this pale lemon frock with a white trim. She'd had it made at some boutique in Collins Street—Lilian at Le Louvre. She wanted me to go back to Melbourne during the war. Not on your nelly. See, I'd only been in Melbourne three weeks, when I came down with the polio. That was 1937. Nine months cooped up in the Alfred Hospital—that was enough.

BRIANNA *and* LYLE *charge in on their bikes.*

BRIANNA: [*looking up*] Are they here yet?

LYLE: [*also looking up*] Well, well, well. Look up there.

NORM *enters* GIRLIE's *memory:*

NORM: I reckon that just might be our girl.

GIRLIE: I reckon that just might be our girl. [*To* BRIANNA] You know, my dad—your great grandpa Norm—was a marvellous pigeon man.

LYLE *exits.*

LYLE: [*as he goes*] You shoulda seen his loft at Allandale.

NORM: It was a beauty all right.

GIRLIE: There was this one time, my dad sold a pair of pigeons to this bloke in the city. And the bloke gets TB and has to go into a sanatorium, see.

NORM: And his missus just opens his cages and lets all his birds go...

GIRLIE: ... every last one of 'em. So one day, I'm with Dad in the yard over at Allandale, and he can tell a pigeon flyin' in the air. What number it is.

NORM: That's 357.

GIRLIE: Even though he sold the bird out of a different loft!

NORM: About twenty-two mile away. In Birchip.

GIRLIE: So that bird lands right at our feet. And he's throwing a bit o' seed around and calling it and that.

NORM: There y'are. 357. Have a look at that. Found its way all the way from Melbourne and to a new loft! See, that girl knew where she belonged.

> NORM *exits.*

GIRLIE: That went on to be a very good pigeon, that one.

BRIANNA: Gran?

GIRLIE: Yes, love?

BRIANNA: Why did Grandpa Norm hang himself?

GIRLIE: I don't know, love. I wish I did.

BRIANNA: Was it because of his pigeons?

GIRLIE: No, darl. Not because of his pigeons.

BRIANNA: Maybe he put in the work and didn't get the rewards.

◆ ◆ ◆ ◆ ◆

SCENE NINETEEN

LYLE *enters the kitchen.* ASHLEIGH *is doing her homework.*

ASHLEIGH: Dad. My friend Anne Cogsley told me that the Hamiltons are going to sell their farm.

> BRIANNA *enters.*

LYLE: Isn't she a sticky-beak.

ASHLEIGH: Her dad's their financial counsellor.

LYLE: Cougar Cogsley. Jesus Christ.

ASHLEIGH: She told me not to tell.

LYLE: That's crook. Spreading your private business all over the district. Bloody hell.

BRIANNA: Would we be able to buy it off them?

LYLE: You wouldn't get me within a hundred mile of one of them, financial counsellors.

BRIANNA: Would we?

He laughs sourly.

LYLE: Got three million dollars, have you? No. If they sell Allandale we're up shit creek.

BRIANNA: But it's our farm.

LYLE: Our farm, Bri. But their land.

BRIANNA: What about Cromies'? That's ours, isn't it?

LYLE: It's only fifteen hundred acres. You can't feed a family on fifteen hundred acres.

MAUREEN *enters.*

MAUREEN: Get a wriggle on, girls. You'll be late for choir.

ASHLEIGH: It's at St Mary's tonight.

MAUREEN: Can you take them? I've got a Progress meeting then I've got to get down to the CFA to get signatures for the petition.

LYLE: The Hamiltons are puttin' Allandale on the market.

Beat.

MAUREEN: I knew this'd bloody happen. I'm going to the solicitor.

LYLE: I said no.

MAUREEN: They're walking all over you, Lyle. It's not fair.

LYLE: Who says life is fair? Life is not fair.

WILLIAM: [*offstage*] Yoo-hoo.

MAUREEN: Oh, Christ. It's the Pansy Boy.

LYLE: He's come for the trestle tables.

WILLIAM: [*offstage*] Hello?

LYLE: We're in here.

WILLIAM: [*entering*] G'day, Maureen. Lyle.

LYLE *goes to the fridge and gets out two tinnies. He pulls the tops off and hands one to* WILLIAM.

LYLE: Hear you're selling the farm.

MAUREEN: I just wrote you people a cheque for six thousand dollars— to run our sheep on land which should be ours.

WILLIAM: What land is that, Maureen?

MAUREEN: You know damn well.

LYLE: Mor—when Nanna Myrtle gave the farm to Aunty Dibs, she gave Mum and Dad ten thousand quid to set them up in the pub.

MAUREEN: Big deal.

LYLE: That was a lot of money sixty years ago.

MAUREEN: The farm is worth two million dollars.

LYLE: And the rest. What with the two houses and the machinery…

MAUREEN: Three million, then.

WILLIAM: Maureen, what has this got to do with you—?

MAUREEN: Lyle has put in more tractor hours than all of yous put together. Every school holiday, every Christmas, every weekend. And you walk back here after thirty years expecting just to clean up.

WILLIAM: Maureen. It's my family's farm.

MAUREEN: Mate, the land belongs to the people who work it. Not to the banks. Not to the multinationals. And certainly not to a pampered city boy who turned tail because he couldn't hack it.

◆ ◆ ◆ ◆ ◆

SCENE TWENTY

GIRLIE *sits on the swing on the front porch sorting through the old suitcase.*

GIRLIE: [*to the audience*] In the end he just couldn't hack it. My dad. It's a mystery to me why a bloke… he had such a lot going for him. Just goes to show, you don't really know anybody, do you?

> GIRLIE *remembers 1934:*

> *Two little girls in blue climb up the fence on the home paddock and watch their father with a water-divining rod.*

YOUNG DIBS: Find one for me, Daddy.

YOUNG GIRLIE: Me too.

GIRLIE: He had a gift. You ask Dibs. He was the dowser found water at Wormie McCallum's place. Good stock water. Saved their farm. Listen to this. 'Dear Mr Myrtle, your divining has been entirely satisfactory. Our bore on the site you have chosen is providing us with gallons of beautiful water. Our windmill will stand as a memorial to your deep penetration of the underground springs.'

GRANDPA NORM's *divining rod begins to shudder and bend. He leans down and picks up something. He strolls over and cleans the dirt off a coin. He hands it to* YOUNG DIBS.

NORM: Here you are, Princess.

YOUNG DIBS: A halfpenny.

The girls look at the halfpenny with awe.

NORM: What year is it?

YOUNG DIBS: 1928.

NORM: Ooh. Crikey O'Reilly. You're in luck. That is a very lucky sign.

YOUNG GIRLIE: Why?

YOUNG DIBS: What is it?

NORM: That was the year Bert Hinkler flew solo from the United Kingdom. In his Avro Avian. February, 1928.

YOUNG GIRLIE: What does it mean?

NORM: It means that your sister (if she plays her cards right) is going to marry a very handsome airman.

YOUNG DIBS: Really?

YOUNG GIRLIE: Can you find one for me? Please? Daddy?

NORM: Hey. Look at that. Under your foot—a Christmas present.

YOUNG DIBS: Gee!

NORM *bends down and picks up another coin.*

NORM: Let's see. On the one side you've got the face of King George the Fifth. That's the face of duty.

YOUNG GIRLIE: Does it say who I'm going to marry?

NORM: And on the back you've got your kangaroo. Bounding about in the bush. A free spirit. Duty or Freedom. Which one will it be?

He tosses the coin in the air.

YOUNG GIRLIE: Freedom.

He shows her the face of the king.

NORM: 'I slept and dreamed that life was beauty; I woke and found that life was Duty.'

YOUNG GIRLIE: Oh?

NORM: That's the hardest lesson in life, I reckon. Accepting how the coin falls and making the best of it.

YOUNG GIRLIE: I want to marry an airman. It's not fair.

NORM: Whoever said life was fair? Life is not fair. See people like me, who always want things to be different—we're the mugs.

The girls sing 'While Shepherds Watch Their Flock By Night'. The church choir builds. The music is dissonant and unhinged.

You look into the face of a big, dumb bullock—are you happy, mate? Do you know something I don't know? Trudging up and down the paddock. Just getting on with it. If I could just stop thinking. Stop this scratching inside my skull. Just work like a big dumb bugger.

CHOIR: [*voice-over, singing*]
        The cattle are lowing,
        The baby awakes…

The sound of the church choir swells, unsettlingly.

DIBS *is at the kitchen table.*

GIRLIE: Do you ever think about Dad?

Monica Maughan (left) as Dibs and Lois Ramsey as Girlie in the 2003 Melbourne Theatre Company production. (Photo: Jeff Busby)

DIBS: Poor old bugger.

CHORUS OF VOICES: [*voice-over*] Ladies and gentlemen, please put your hands together…

Find one for me, Daddy…

That went on to be a very good pigeon that one…

Does it say who I'm gonna marry…?

I reckon that just might be our girl…

… for the winners of the 1934 Norm Myrtle Trophy…

The music is a cacophony of Christmas carols as the two little girls run across the yard holding toys and Christmas wrapping.

YOUNG DIBS: Dad? Dad?

YOUNG GIRLIE: Father Christmas has been!

CHOIR: [*voice-over, singing*]

I love Thee, Lord Jesus, look down from the sky!

They push open the woolshed door at the back of the stage. NORM, *half-dressed in his Father Christmas suit, is swinging from the rafters. The little girls scream.*

Silence.

GIRLIE *is alone with the suitcase, she is holding the Father Christmas beard and hat. She bends down and picks a coin off the ground.*

GIRLIE: Crikey O'Reilly, Girl. You're in luck. That is a very lucky sign.

◆ ◆ ◆ ◆ ◆

SCENE TWENTY-ONE

The Hamiltons' yard.

There is a toot-tooting of the horn. Dogs go berserk. WILLIAM, FARLEY *and* DIBS *gather to greet them.*

FARLEY: [*to* DIBS] Who's this now?

DIBS: It's Julia, darling. Julia.

JULIA: Hi.

NUGGET: Burke and Wills are here.

JULIA: Hi, Dad.

WILLIAM: The prodigals return.

DIBS: Thanks awfully, Nuggs.

NUGGET: No worries.

FARLEY: [*to* WILLIAM] That your wife, is it?

WILLIAM: No. I don't have a wife.

FELIX: Hi, Grandpa.

JULIA: Happy birthday, Mum.

FARLEY: [*to the dogs*] Git on there, Blackie! G'on!

WILLIAM: G'day, Felix.

FELIX: Uncle Will.

WILLIAM: Welcome to the Funny Farm.

FARLEY: [*to the dogs*] Out! Out! Get lost, you sneaky bugger!

WILLIAM: How are you, darling?

JULIA: Hot as hell.

FELIX: Hi, Nanna Dibs. Happy birthday.

DIBS: [*hugging* FELIX] How lovely that you could come, when I know you're so busy.

WILLIAM: Where's the car?

DIBS: What's this?

NUGGET: The rope broke.

FELIX: The cake, I think.

JULIA: On the Ultima Road.

NUGGET: Just before the 'Golla turnoff.

The family are all bundled indoors, when FARLEY *turns to* NUGGET.

FARLEY: Nugget. Those eight hundred wethers are ready for the boat.

NUGGET: Yep. We'll get them off to Portland tomorrow. Don't you worry.

FARLEY *exits.*

WILLIAM: [*to* NUGGET] We don't have any wethers, do we?

NUGGET: Nup.

NUGGET *goes indoors.* WILLIAM *and* JULIA *remain on the verandah.*

WILLIAM: You're looking very…

JULIA: What?

WILLIAM: … rosy-cheeked.

JULIA: Must be the country air.

WILLIAM: You're not in love, are you?

> JULIA *smiles enigmatically. Pause.*

I saw your ex-husband last week. He came into the restaurant.

JULIA: Is he really fat?

WILLIAM: He is, rather.

JULIA: Good.

WILLIAM: He seemed to think you were going out with an Indian gentleman.

JULIA: I want to know what you're up to.

WILLIAM: What do you mean?

JULIA: You've been up here three weekends in a row.

WILLIAM: I'm worried about Mum.

JULIA: Why?

WILLIAM: He's gone completely ga-ga. Last week he lost the tractor.

JULIA: Nugget found it.

WILLIAM: That's not the point.

JULIA: She doesn't want to put him into an old people's home.

WILLIAM: You only get one life and she's lived hers with a tyrant.

JULIA: He can't help it.

WILLIAM: I just want her to be rid of him. But this bloody farm has been a noose around her neck for sixty years. You've got to support me on this. She won't do it unless we help her.

JULIA: I don't want her to sell, Will. I think it's a mistake. She'll never cope. And what about Nugget? What's he going to do? Anyway, I love coming up here.

WILLIAM: This is not about what's good for you.

◆ ◆ ◆ ◆ ◆

SCENE TWENTY-TWO

The Delaneys' kitchen.

ASHLEIGH *is doing her homework.* BRIANNA *is painting a sign that says* 'Banks for People'.

MAUREEN: What about Nugget?

LYLE: What about him?

MAUREEN: I wouldn't put it past Farley to leave the farm to him. He's going soft in the head.

LYLE: I don't think so, Mor.

MAUREEN: Mind you, that'd be letting the cat out of the bag.

> LYLE *clears his throat sharply to warn against speaking in front of the girls.*

Oh, for chrissake. They keep up this front of bein' a cut above everybody else, those Hamiltons. With their private school voices and university education and period furniture. (Jeez, I hate that stuff.) But no one ever says anything about—

LYLE: Maureen! Please!

ASHLEIGH: About what?

LYLE: Never you mind.

ASHLEIGH: Mum?

MAUREEN: Homework, Big Ears.

> *Silence.* GIRLIE *enters.*

ASHLEIGH: What do coons mean when they say the land is 'my mother'?

BRIANNA: Don't call them that!

ASHLEIGH: What?

LYLE: It's like us saying we believe in the Easter Bunny.

MAUREEN: Except the Easter Bunny doesn't qualify you to get millions of acres of Crown Land.

BRIANNA: That's just racist. Yous are so racist.

MAUREEN: Look. Aboriginal people themselves don't all believe that stuff. It's your university types and do-gooders from the city, they're

the ones who keep peddling this tribal oogy-boogy. And most of
'em have never even clapped eyes on an Aboriginal.

GIRLIE: All I know is, we had some eggheads up here, from the university.
This is back when we had the pub. They were doing this research on
Aboriginal history in the district. I said, 'You should talk to my
nephew, Nugget. He's an Aboriginal.'

MAUREEN: Oh, quick as you like, this young fella, his eyes lit up. 'He
must be one of the stolen generation', he says. Rubbing his hands
together.

GIRLIE: Stolen, my arse. Nugget's mother was killed in a road smash. It
was a tragedy. And my sister Dibs—who's the most Christian woman
you'd ever meet—took on this young boy. In fact she adopted him
and looked after him like he was one of her own. And he's a good
boy, Nugget. He's done them proud. Mind you, it hasn't been all
beer and skittles. They've had their rough patches.

MAUREEN: But they come round here, these university types, askin' the
cockies if they've found any 'artefacts' on their land—you know,
Aboriginal axe heads, flints, bones and that. I shouldn't say too much—

She goes inside.

GIRLIE: Wasting their time. Nobody in this district has ever found anything
at all. And even if you had, you wouldn't tell the bloody Mabo mob,
would you?

◆ ◆ ◆ ◆ ◆

SCENE TWENTY-THREE

The Hamiltons'.

FELIX *enters the kitchen wearing a t-shirt with 'Sorry' emblazoned over
the front.* FARLEY *is sitting with an old sheet draped across him. He and*
NUGGET *are having a mug of tea and some of Dibs' scones.*

FELIX: You seen Mum?

NUGGET: Nup. Hey, Felix, what is it you're studying at university?

FELIX: Cyber societies.

NUGGET *roars laughing.*

NUGGET: Cyber societies. That's a killer.

There is a click.

FELIX: Ooh.

NUGGET: Snap.

FARLEY: There goes another one. Grab it, will you?

FELIX: What?

FARLEY: The mousetrap.

FELIX: Ugh, Jesus.

NUGGET: I'll do it.

FARLEY: Stay where you are! [*To* FELIX] He'll do it.

Pause.

FELIX: Do what?

FARLEY: Dispose of the mouse.

NUGGET: Here, I don't mind—

FARLEY: [*to* NUGGET] Sit down!

FELIX: Do I just chuck it away?

FARLEY: You weak little git. [*Slowly*] Dispose of the mouse and then reset the trap.

FELIX *picks up the mousetrap and walks out of the room, watched by the two men.*

NUGGET: Come on. Let's get stuck into this. Tidy you up for the party, eh?

NUGGET *brandishes a pair of hair-cutting scissors.*

FARLEY: Lot o' fuss about bugger all.

NUGGET: Still, can't have you lookin' like Archie Kirkwood.

FARLEY *laughs despite himself.*

'Can anyone smell burning?'

FARLEY *and* NUGGET *crack up. Soon they are laughing so hard they are struggling to get words out.*

FARLEY: And then... and then... and then... who was it?

NUGGET: Lucky Joe.

FARLEY: Lucky Joe tipped that whole jug of Vic Bitter—
NUGGET: On Archie's head.
FARLEY: I thought the poor prick was gonna go up in flames.

> *Eventually they recover, wiping tears from their eyes.*

What's all this again?
NUGGET: It's Mum's birthday, tomorrow. And you bought her a beautiful
pearl necklace.
FARLEY: Did I?
NUGGET: You did. We went into Swan Hill together last week.
FARLEY: Where'd I put it, d'you reckon?
NUGGET: I'm lookin' after it. Don't you worry.

> FARLEY *takes this in.*

FARLEY: Is Lucky Joe coming?
NUGGET: He's in the ground, mate.
FARLEY: That'd be right. We've buried all the good ones.
NUGGET: Thought you hated Micks.
FARLEY: Do I?

> *He reaches up and grasps* NUGGET*'s hand, gripped by a moment
> of terror.*

Don't let them take me. I'm going mad.
NUGGET: I'm lookin' out for you. Don't worry.

> NUGGET *looks out the window.*

FARLEY: You've got to be big to own country like this.

> *He squeezes* NUGGET*'s hand even tighter.*

◆ ◆ ◆ ◆ ◆

SCENE TWENTY-FOUR

GIRLIE: [*to the audience*] You've got to have a sense of humour to live
in country like this. I wish you could've met my husband, Lucky
Joe. He was such a funny man. You know you're blessed if you've
found a bloke who can make you laugh.

GIRLIE *enters her memory:*

A dance. 1937. All the couples are dancing. JOE DELANEY *enters the hall with* LOFTY BLAKE.

JOE: Don't get me started, Lofty. Never tell your private business to a Presbyterian.

LOFTY: Why's that, Joe?

JOE: I was talking to Reverend Beecher. I was telling him that we were doing a bit of catering on the side for weddings. And blow me down if one week later the Presbyterian Ladies Guild weren't advertising that they cater for weddings. They get Mrs Bradley to bring a sponge and Mrs Piper to do a trifle. I was getting a guinea and they were doing it for twelve-and-six. Cut the guts out of the job for us.

LOFTY: Cripes.

JOE: You can't fight those Presbyterian sheilas.

> *He notices* GIRLIE.

Who's that?

LOFTY: Girlie Myrtle.

JOE: Girlie Myrtle. She's a bit of all right.

LOFTY: She can't walk.

JOE: Why not?

LOFTY: Polio.

JOE: Can't walk don't mean you can't dance.

> *He makes his way over to* GIRLIE.

I wonder if I might have the pleasure?

GIRLIE: What?

JOE: I'd like to have a dance?

GIRLIE: Sorry. I don't dance.

JOE: Good. Then you won't show me up.

GIRLIE: Nah. Really.

JOE: I've come all the way from Warracknabeal.

> *He picks her up and glides her around the room.*

I'm Joe Delaney, by the way.

GIRLIE: Are you just?

JOE: I know who you are.

GIRLIE: How come?

JOE: I made it my business to find out.

They do a circle of the room.

GIRLIE: Thanks for makin' a fool of me.

JOE: Are you kidding? I'm the envy of every fella in this room.

◆ ◆ ◆ ◆ ◆

SCENE TWENTY-FIVE

The Hamiltons' shed.

NUGGET *and* FARLEY *are setting up trestle tables.*

NUGGET: He was a good bloke, Lucky Joe. He won the Stawell Gift, you know. Before the war or something.

FARLEY: Did he?

NUGGET: So he reckons. He used to drive the baker's cart and he'd run alongside it for the last fifteen mile. That's how he trained.

FARLEY: Is that so?

NUGGET: He told me he borrowed five quid from everyone he knew and he backed himself on the race. He made eight hundred quid on top of the prize money.

FARLEY: I don't remember.

NUGGET: You're all right.

LYLE *enters with a keg on a trolley. He's been drinking.*

LYLE: Here's the important gear.

NUGGET: Good on you, mate. Park him over there.

LYLE *stumbles and loses the keg.*

You all right, mate?

FARLEY: Never put a Mick in charge of anything.

NUGGET: Come on, you old Presbyterian, give us a hand with these.

FARLEY: Think like peasants.

LYLE: What was that?

NUGGET: Don't worry about it, mate.

FARLEY: Bloody bog Irish.

NUGGET: Okay, matey.

FARLEY: In the grip of the priests.

NUGGET: Here. Other end. Dad?

FARLEY: Always got on in the public service, you know. The Micks.

LYLE: I've had it with this crap.

NUGGET: Mate, he's an old man.

FARLEY: They couldn't come to our wedding—Lucky Joe and them. Priests won't let 'em go into anyone else's church. 'Cause they're frightened they'll see the light.

NUGGET: Hey! [*To* FARLEY] Grab the other two trestles.

> FARLEY *busies himself unfolding the trestles.* NUGGET *helps* LYLE *get the keg set up.*

LYLE: Mate. 'Bout that seeder?

NUGGET: You never give up, do you?

LYLE: Mate. I've been talkin' to the finance mob. They've done us a deal. On a crop lien.

NUGGET: Not me, mate. Count me out.

LYLE: Take a risk for once in your life.

NUGGET: You're in over your neck.

LYLE: You reckon you're runnin' things, but you're just a fuckin' farm hand.

NUGGET: I'm not buyin' the seeder, Lyle.

LYLE: It's crap anyway. They're selling the farm.

NUGGET: What?

LYLE: So we're both up shit creek.

FARLEY: What's he saying?

NUGGET: He's full of bullshit. C'mon, Dad. Let's go up to the house.

> *They leave.* LYLE *taps himself a beer.*

LYLE: [*muttering*] Bloody boong. Never had to stand on your own two feet, you black bastard.

> DIBS *enters with plates.*

DIBS: That wind could turn nasty, Lyle.

LYLE: Could do. [*Offering* DIBS *a beer*] Hey, how about it, Aunty Dibs?

DIBS: I think I might save myself for tomorrow, love.

LYLE: Any rate, I reckon we should think carefully about that seeder.

DIBS: Oh, Lyle, we've been through this, darl.

LYLE: Have a quiet word with Crash Thompson. Get a second opinion. He's a bloke who really knows his onions.

DIBS: Nugget's done his costings, love, and it's just not worth our while.

LYLE: His lot aren't great on farm management, Aunty Dibs.

DIBS: He went to Longerenong, Lyle. He's got a Diploma of Agriculture.

LYLE: They're not worth the paper they're printed on. No one can teach you to be a farmer. It's either in you or it isn't. He was bleatin' on the other day, that I was overstocked. What a joke.

DIBS: Your place does look a bit bare, darl.

LYLE: Every blade of grass standing in the paddock is money goin' to waste.

DIBS: Is that so?

LYLE: Your pasture's not workin' for ya till it's inside a sheep's stomach. I'm telling ya, Aunty Dibs, Nugget's a great bloke and that, but they make hopeless bloody farmers.

DIBS: Lyle. Go home. Sober up.

◆ ◆ ◆ ◆ ◆

SCENE TWENTY-SIX

Main Street, Rushton.

GIRLIE *and* MAUREEN *have set themselves up with a card table outside the Rushton CFA. They are seeking signatures for a petition for a rural transaction centre.* JULIA, FELIX *and* WILLIAM *are walking along.*

JULIA: The town's so empty, isn't it?

FELIX: Spooky.

JULIA: Do you feel anything? Anything at all?

WILLIAM: I feel anxious that my car might break down and I'd be stuck here. See that empty block up there—behind Delaney's pub. I lost my virginity in the back of a VW, there. With Fingers McClure.

JULIA: William was regarded as quite a stud, back then.

WILLIAM: A stud with a guilty secret.

FELIX: Did you call her 'Fingers' to her face?

WILLIAM: No. Beverley. Anyway, she wouldn't let me touch her boosies.

JULIA: Quite right too.

WILLIAM: But when I finally got to take her bra off, out came handfuls of cotton wool. Handfuls! Stuffed down there. It was terrifying.

JULIA: Hey, is that Maureen up there?

WILLIAM: Quick. Nip down here.

JULIA: No! We can't. She's seen us.

WILLIAM: Shit!

JULIA: [waving] Hi, Maureen!

MAUREEN: Hi! [To GIRLIE] It's whining Julia and the Pansy Boy.

GIRLIE: Is that Felix? He's a weedy-looking bloke, isn't he? I see what you mean. He does look like a fairy.

JULIA: Hi, Aunty Girl. How are you? Felix, you remember Aunty Girl, don't you?

FELIX: Hey.

MAUREEN: Hello, yous. Come to sign our petition, have you?

JULIA: What is it?

MAUREEN: We're trying to get a rural transaction centre in the milk bar.

GIRLIE: Since we've lost the bank and the post office. How are you, Will?

WILLIAM: Well, thanks, Aunty Girl.

MAUREEN: They reckon we're too small, but we'll see about that.

GIRLIE: They all go into Swan Hill o' course. Do their business in there.

MAUREEN: [pointing] Poor ol' Archie here.

GIRLIE: Everyone shops at Safeway in Swan Hill.

MAUREEN: And on the way home, with two hundred bucks worth of groceries in the boot, they realise they've forgotten bread or milk or something—so they stop at Archie's and put it on the tab. It's not right.

GIRLIE: He can't keep going.

FELIX: That's globalisation for you.

GIRLIE: She's going into politics, you know.

JULIA: Mum said.

GIRLIE: Can't be any more stupid than Roly Pigget.

FELIX: Who's he? Your local member?

GIRLIE: There was a time when you could've put a chook in the National Party and people round here woulda voted for it. But not anymore.

MAUREEN: So what's happening about Allandale? Any more news?

JULIA: What about?

MAUREEN: Doesn't she know?

GIRLIE: What?

MAUREEN: William?

WILLIAM: I don't know any more than you do, Maureen.

JULIA: What's this?

From left: Julie Nihill as Julia, Rhys McConnochie as William, Geraldine Turner as Maureen and Lois Ramsey as Girlie in the 2003 Melbourne Theatre Company production. (Photo: Jeff Busby)

MAUREEN: It's all over town.

JULIA: What?

MAUREEN: Your mother's putting Allandale on the market.

GIRLIE: Over my dead body she is.

JULIA: I think you might have got the wrong end of the stick.

MAUREEN: I hope so. I really hope so. Otherwise things might get very
nasty around here.

Beat. GIRLIE *remembers:*

It is 1938. YOUNG GIRLIE *and* YOUNG DIBS *are sitting on a fence at
the farm, surveying the land.*

YOUNG GIRLIE: One of us has got to stay. [*Long pause.*] Agreed?

YOUNG DIBS: But what about my nursing? I love being down in
Melbourne, Girl. It's everything I've always dreamed of. And Dulcie
and me, we're thinking of getting a flat.

YOUNG GIRLIE: One of us takes on the farm and the other is free to go.
[*Long pause.*] Right?

YOUNG DIBS: What about Lucky Joe?

YOUNG GIRLIE: He's taking over the Rushton pub.

YOUNG DIBS: And that's where you want to live, is it? In a hotel?

YOUNG GIRLIE: He's asked me to marry him.

YOUNG DIBS: Remember what Dad used to say, 'You can tell a Catholic by
his eyes'. He'd turn in his grave, Girl.

YOUNG GIRLIE: As if I care two hoots about what our father might damn
well think. As if he ever gave us a thought, when he strung himself
up. That's a sin against God, what he did. And I was punished for it.
With the polio.

Pause.

YOUNG DIBS: Someone has to look after Mum.

YOUNG GIRLIE: That's right. This is the only fair way.

YOUNG DIBS: I suppose so.

YOUNG GIRLIE: King George or the kangaroo?

YOUNG DIBS: Duty or Freedom.

YOUNG GIRLIE: Heads or tails?

YOUNG DIBS: Heads.

YOUNG GIRLIE: Heads, you get the farm.

> *She tosses the coin high up into the sky. Both* GIRLIE *and* MAUREEN *look up into the sky.*

> GIRLIE *is disturbed from her reverie. The wind is stirring and the corrugated iron sheeting on a nearby disused shop is rattling.*

MAUREEN: I think we might be in for a dust storm.

GIRLIE: See you later, all right.

MAUREEN: Where are you going?

GIRLIE: I need to have a talk with my sister.

◆ ◆ ◆ ◆ ◆

SCENE TWENTY-SEVEN

The Hamiltons' dining room.

They are about to eat dinner.

JULIA: Mum, Maureen said you were selling the farm. That's bullshit, isn't it?

DIBS: Sweetheart, please.

JULIA: What?

DIBS: That language. You know it bothers me.

JULIA: Everybody's talking about it in town.

DIBS: You just sound so c-o-double m-o-n [*common*].

JULIA: You wouldn't sell up without discussing it with me, would you?

DIBS: No, darling.

JULIA: I'd be completely devastated.

DIBS: Oh, come on, darling.

JULIA: What?

DIBS: I'm sure you'd deal with it perfectly well.

JULIA: No, I wouldn't.

DIBS: You're very adaptable. It's one of your… qualities.

JULIA: Mum, I want to set up a business here. I've been doing research. I want to start a herb farm. And I'm going to grow tomatoes.

Remember that year we planted them over the septic tank and we got a tonne. And we bottled them. And they were so delicious. Don't you remember?

DIBS: Here, set these out [*plates*], would you?

JULIA: I am really serious about this. [*Pause.*] My circumstances have changed…

DIBS: You haven't lost your job?

JULIA: No.

DIBS: Thank goodness for that. It wouldn't have mattered so much if Hamish were still on the scene. But… unfortunately…

JULIA: I'm seeing someone else.

DIBS: I expected you would be. You're not one to let the grass grow under your feet.

> DIBS *rings the bell.*

JULIA: Why won't you take this seriously?

DIBS: Sweetie, there are a collection of half-knitted jumpers in that cupboard in there. Skirts that you've cut out and never sewn.

JULIA: So?

DIBS: Don't let's have a fight. I just know that you're not good on the follow-up. Seeing things through.

JULIA: I am an adult.

> WILLIAM *enters.*

WILLIAM: Really? Since when?

JULIA: Shut up, Will!

DIBS: Julia!

JULIA: I am not the little girl who comes home from boarding school anymore.

DIBS: First there was the water bed business. Then there was the Moroccan jewellery. And then you had some idea about printing ironing board covers with humorous messages.

> FELIX, NUGGET *and* FARLEY *enter.*

JULIA: Mum, I have been working in the public service for twelve years.

DIBS: And that's what you're good at. Come on, let's sit down.

JULIA: I don't want to do it anymore.

DIBS: Will, can you go in next to Daddy? Felix, darling, you're here. Doesn't Julia look radiant?

NUGGET: I'll say. Radiant.

DIBS: Felix, would you say grace?

    FELIX *looks completely horrified.* NUGGET *grins.*

NUGGET: I'll do it.

DIBS: Thanks, Nugget.

NUGGET: Perhaps we could say a little Hindu prayer.

    FELIX *giggles.*

DIBS: Why's that, Nuggs?

FARLEY: Hurry up. Get on with it, will you?

FELIX: I think Mum's got a bit of news she'd like to share with you.

JULIA: No, I haven't.

NUGGET: I think you might have.

JULIA: How do you know?

    She glares at FELIX, *who looks at her innocently.*

FARLEY: Come on. It's getting cold.

NUGGET: For what we are about to receive may the Lord make us truly thankful. Amen.

    Suddenly there is the sound of tyres on the gravel and a loud honking from the driveway outside.

DIBS: Who's this, then?

    NUGGET *looks out the window.*

WILLIAM: It's Aunty Girl.

DIBS: Oh, lord.

    GIRLIE *rides up defiantly on her converted motor-mower.*

NUGGET: Nice set of wheels, Auntie Girl.

DIBS: Girlie, what are you thinking!?

GIRLIE: This is not fair, Dibs—what you're doing. Here, William. Give us a hand, will you?

WILLIAM: How do you switch it off?

NUGGET: Give us a look.

GIRLIE: We have to make a decision about the farm. My children need to know where they stand.

DIBS: Honestly, Girl! What's got into you?

GIRLIE: It's all over town. The whole district knows.

NUGGET: Knows what?

GIRLIE: That you're selling.

FARLEY: What are they selling?

DIBS: Ssh, love. Eat your tea.

GIRLIE: You didn't bother to say anything to us. Your own family.

NUGGET: Someone's spreading rumours.

WILLIAM: Let's not get too emotional.

GIRLIE: This is what happens when you tell your business to Cougar Cogsley.

WILLIAM: The key issue for Mum is that she is going to have to get some help with a certain person. Eventually.

Lois Ramsey as Girlie and Ronald Falk as Farley in the 2003 Melbourne Theatre Company production. (Photo: Jeff Busby)

GIRLIE: I understand that.

WILLIAM: I don't think you do. She can't keep living out here. She needs to be close to the doctor—

GIRLIE: What's wrong with Swan Hill? They got doctors.

DIBS: I don't like Swan Hill.

GIRLIE: It's a damn sight better than Melbourne.

DIBS: I love Melbourne.

GIRLIE: Don't tell me you're thinking of moving to that stinking hole?

FARLEY: We're not moving anywhere. You tell them, Mum. We'll be dead and gone before anyone's doing any moving.

DIBS: That's right, love. Can we talk about this later?

GIRLIE: You'd never be able to afford anything half-way decent in Melbourne. Two hundred thousand wouldn't get you a shoe box. And before you know it, they've locked you up in one of those rest homes and some little Asiatic nurse is scrubbing you down with kerosene.

JULIA: Girlie!

DIBS: Honestly.

GIRLIE: Once they stick you in one of those places you never get out alive.

DIBS: I am not planning to go to a rest home.

GIRLIE: What are you planning, then?

> *Pause.*

DIBS: Pass the beans will you, Felix?

> *Pause.*

WILLIAM: We're thinking of buying a vineyard.

JULIA: Who's we?

WILLIAM: Kevin and I. And possibly Mum.

JULIA: [*to* DIBS] You haven't said anything about this to me.

WILLIAM: We're going to sell the restaurant and open a new one on this incredibly beautiful property.

DIBS: On the Mornington Peninsula.

GIRLIE: [*to* DIBS] And what's this got to do with you?

WILLIAM: We thought… a certain person… might like to come too.

FELIX: Grandpa?

JULIA: No. Ssh.

GIRLIE: He wants you to live with him, does he? With the boyfriend.

DIBS: Of course not.

WILLIAM: The boyfriend has a name.

FELIX: Kevin.

WILLIAM: Mum would have her own brand new home, which she's dreamt of—all her life. Which she can design to her own specifications.

JULIA: You'd build?

GIRLIE: Build? Don't be stupid. Laurie Bagot was dead before they got the roof on.

The sound of tyres on the gravel again. NUGGET *looks out.*

NUGGET: Lyle and Maureen.

DIBS: Oh, my godfather.

JULIA: That's all we need.

GIRLIE: They slugged him for twice as much as the original quote.

DIBS: Get some more chairs please, Felix.

GIRLIE: They're thieves down there—the builders and that. They'll see you coming a mile off.

FARLEY: What are you talking about?

MAUREEN: Hello all. Sorry to barge in like this.

LYLE: We've brought down the seats from the hall.

JULIA: Hello, Ashleigh. Hi, Bri.

ASHLEIGH & BRIANNA: [*together*] Hi.

FARLEY: [*distressed*] Who are these people?

DIBS: Come on, love.

FARLEY: Are they going soon?

DIBS: Let's take our tea out here to the kitchen. Excuse us.

JULIA: Mum, sit down. Felix, why don't you take Grandpa?

FELIX: Do I have to?

JULIA: Yes.

MAUREEN: Ashleigh—take Grandpa's plate, please.

GIRLIE: Sit down, Dibs. Let Maureen.

MAUREEN: [*to* FARLEY] We'll get you out to the kitchen, eh, where it's a bit quieter and you can eat your tea in peace. Here we go. That's the way. Brianna. Help me here please.

MAUREEN *exits with* FARLEY *and the girls.*

JULIA: Felix!?

FELIX: What? Get off my case.

GIRLIE: So, how are you intending to pay for this brand new home then? [*Pause.*] Dibs? That's what I want to know.

NUGGET: You wouldn't sell this place, would you, Mum?

GIRLIE: That's out of the question.

DIBS: It's my decision. [*Pause.*] Mine and Farley's.

GIRLIE: Farley is incapable of making a decision. And no matter what you say, this farm does not belong to Farley. He's made a damn good living out of it. But it is not his land.

JULIA: What do you mean by that?

GIRLIE: It was not his grandmother came across from Pinnaroo.

DIBS: Oh, for heaven's sake.

GIRLIE: No. Bugger you. It wasn't his people broke their backs clearing this country. It was our grandmother, Jessie Allan. And she didn't call it Allandale so some freeloader could just walk in.

DIBS: Freeloader? What's got into you?

NUGGET: This is his farm.

GIRLIE: This is a matter for family, I'm afraid.

JULIA: How dare you say that!

NUGGET: This is Farley Hamilton's farm.

DIBS: Calm down, Nugget.

WILLIAM: The farm belongs to Mum.

DIBS: It's Farley's name on the title.

WILLIAM: What?

GIRLIE: That means bugger all.

NUGGET: Farley's worked it all his life.

LYLE: I'd pipe down if I were you.

JULIA: Nugget has more right to speak in this house than anyone.

LYLE: Not when it comes to this farm, he doesn't.

NUGGET: Excuse me?!

LYLE: He's not in line.

JULIA: Says who?

NUGGET: Bugger off, Lyle. You're embarrassing yourself.

LYLE: Mate, you're the embarrassment.

GIRLIE: Steady, Lyle.

LYLE: You're a joke, mate.

WILLIAM: That's enough.

LYLE: A laughing stock.

NUGGET: Piss off.

JULIA: Jesus, Lyle.

GIRLIE: [*calling offstage*] Maureen!

LYLE: This farm is going down the bloody gurgler.

NUGGET: Come on, you. Out. Out.

DIBS: He's had too much to drink.

LYLE: Just a bloody excuse for a farmer.

> MAUREEN *re-enters.*

NUGGET: Out.

GIRLIE: Maureen, take him home, will you?

DIBS: He's had a skinful.

MAUREEN: Oh, Christ.

LYLE: It's not me that's pissed.

MAUREEN: [*calling*] Girls!

NUGGET: Lyle, get out.

MAUREEN: [*calling*] Girls!

> BRIANNA *and* ASHLEIGH *re-enter.*

LYLE: You're a cunning bastard, I'll give you that.

MAUREEN: [*to the girls*] In the car.

NUGGET: What are you on about?

LYLE: Welchin' on the fuckin' deal.

> NUGGET *hauls* LYLE *outside.* MAUREEN *and the girls exit with them.*
> *Pause.*

GIRLIE: I know you think you won the farm with the toss of a coin.

DIBS: Oh, Girlie. We were children.

GIRLIE: We were eighteen. We tossed a coin. You won this farm on the
flip of a coin.

DIBS: Oh, come on.

GIRLIE: I've honoured that all my life, Dibs. But that toss is not binding on our kids. They have to be free of that.

DIBS: Girlie, our mother gave you ten thousand pounds.

GIRLIE: Our mother did what you told her. There you were with your fighter pilot. Wing-Commander Farley Hamilton in his flash uniform and his big moustache. She thought he was Christmas, so she signed over everything—

DIBS: She gave you ten thousands pounds.

GIRLIE: It's not land.

DIBS: But you were able to buy the pub.

GIRLIE: But you got the farm.

DIBS: I never wanted the farm.

GIRLIE: Well, give it to someone who does. This farm stays in the family. It's a question of blood. Allandale belongs to Lyle.

> *There is an ear-piercing scream from* MAUREEN. ASHLEIGH *runs in.*

ASHLEIGH: They're fighting!

◆ ◆ ◆ ◆ ◆

SCENE TWENTY-EIGHT

The Hamiltons'.

The family rush out to see NUGGET *and* LYLE *rolling around in the red dirt. The fight is vicious and frightening. Dogs are barking wildly.* NUGGET *has got blood streaming down his face.* LYLE *grabs a shovel and aims a couple of blows at* NUGGET.

LYLE: Fucking bastard. Fucking shit-arse coon.

DIBS: Stop this at once.

GIRLIE: Both of yous.

> NUGGET *gets the advantage and lays into* LYLE.

NUGGET: Don't you ever call me coon. You understand?

LYLE: Suits me, you black cunt.

NUGGET: Stop this, Lyle. I don't want to fucking hurt you.

LYLE: You pissweak coon.

> NUGGET *shoves* LYLE *who falls to the ground.* NUGGET *grabs the spade and, as he brings it down,* LYLE *rolls out of the way and the spade slams onto his hand.* LYLE *screams.*
>
> *Blackout.*

END OF ACT ONE

ACT TWO

SCENE ONE

The Rushton Agricultural and Pastoral Show. (A&P Society Show) There are all the sound effects of fairground music, children squealing on the Ferris wheel and a muffled loud-speaker announcing missing children, the results of the sheep-dog trials and the preserves display in the pavilion. The Grand Parade will be at 3pm.

PUBLIC ADDRESS: [*voice-over*] Could someone please bring the results of the showjumping to the stewards' stand in the middle of the arena. Thank you.

And now, ladies and gentlemen, here's a little lady with a lot to say for herself. They're calling her the 'Mouth of the Mallee'. Please welcome the Independent candidate for Murray—Maureen Delaney.

The back doors roll open. Accompanied by triumphal music, her campaign song 'Lend A Hand'*, MAUREEN DELANEY *rides in on the back of a ute which rolls down the stage towards the audience. She is waving to the crowd of enthusiastic supporters who clap and whistle and stamp their feet (on the sound track). A large banner reads:*

> *'Vote One Maureen Delaney*
> *Putting the Mallee First'*

MAUREEN *addresses the assembled crowd.*

MAUREEN: Thank you. Thank you. Thank you. Ladies and gentlemen. I was born in the Mallee. I went to school here. I got my first job at Dobsons' in Swan Hill. This is where I've raised my family. And I know what it means to work my guts out. I know Mallee people and I'm telling you right now, we've got a problem.

---

* 'Lend A Hand', words and music by Ian McDonald and Michael Cathcart (see appendix at end of playtext).

Geraldine Turner as Maureen in the 2003 Melbourne Theatre Company production. (Photo: Jeff Busby)

Do you know why some of us can't get the phone to work? Why we drive every day on roads that are not safe? Why our children are being educated in second-rate schools? Do you? I'll tell you why. We're too bloody nice. That's why. We're too decent. Let's get one thing straight. You deserve—your kids deserve—the same basic facilities as city people take for granted. But have you got a problem sticking up for yourself, or what?

Let me tell you a true story. One night, a gang of bikies come hooning into Rushton. Stirring up trouble, making a helluva racket. I had this young fella working with me in the pub and he says to me, 'Maureen,' he says, 'they're gonna trash this place'. And I thought, 'Bugger that. I am not going to be intimidated by a band of thugs.' So I march over to this big hairy bloke in a leather vest with tatts all over him and I say, 'Out!' I say, 'You heard me. On yer bike. Now!' He stares at me long and hard, this creep and then he says, 'Yes, ma'am'. And he gives me a little bow and they get on their bikes and ride out of town. True story.

My friends, we made this country. And we're not about to be bullied by foreign interests who are no different to those bikies. I'm talking about the multinationals. I'm talking about the foreign-owned banks. And I'm talking about every Asian, Moslem and Hottentot who come here and refuse to sign up to the Australian Way of Life. There are women who come to this country who are not prepared to show their faces. Well I say, 'Don't show your face around here'. My friends, this is Australia, where people say g'day to each other in the street and lend a hand when they see a mate in trouble.

You know me. I'm Maureen Delaney. On Election Day—put the Mallee first. Put a *One* beside Maureen Delaney.

◆ ◆ ◆ ◆ ◆

SCENE TWO

A coffin is carried across the stage.

◆ ◆ ◆ ◆ ◆

SCENE THREE

The family gather at the cemetery gate.

DIBS, GIRLIE, WILLIAM *and six-month-pregnant* JULIA *stand together looking out at the cemetery and surrounding country.* FELIX *and the two girls stand to one side—in black.* NUGGET *stands alone.*

A long silence.

WILLIAM: You sure you told the minister the right cemetery?

JULIA: Maybe he went to Chinkapook.

WILLIAM: It's only twenty-five bucks for a plot over there.

GIRLIE: And they throw in afternoon tea.

JULIA: But you have to dig the grave yourself.

DIBS: Honestly.

GIRLIE: The Presbyterian section's full anyway.

WILLIAM: He could have bunked in with the Micks.

DIBS: Will.

◆ ◆ ◆

GIRLIE: Remember your wedding? Farley in his officer's uniform. At Scots' Church. With all those boys in their Airforce clobber.

DIBS: [*to* JULIA] We had dinner at the Oriental Hotel afterwards. In Collins Street. It was like a Somerset Maugham novel. Potted plants, and black-and-white marble tiles in the entrance—

GIRLIE: —and three violinists were playing.

> *Music from 'Harbour Lights'*.*

It was the happiest I ever saw him.

DIBS: Then he got the telegram. The very next morning. Telling him to report to Sydney.

GIRLIE: His squadron was flying north to the war in the Pacific.

---

* 'Harbour Lights', words and music by Jimmy Kennedy and Hugh Williams.

DIBS: I went up with him on the overnight train. It was full of troops, squashed along the corridors. We booked into this funny old-fashioned hotel—the Continental—with a shaky wire cage for a lift. And then we said goodbye on the Harbour Bridge. I found my way back to the hotel and I lay on the bed and cried myself to sleep. I don't know how long I slept, but when I woke up it was dark and someone was banging on the door! It was Farley shouting, 'Open up! Open up! I've got ten days! I've got ten days leave!'

The music stops.

[*To* JULIA] I wish you could have known him then.

Silence.

◆ ◆ ◆

JULIA: Dad used to say it was the silence that kept him here.
DIBS: He never wanted to be a farmer.
GIRLIE: We all got trapped into doing things we didn't want to do.

Pause.

◆ ◆ ◆

MAUREEN *and* LYLE *arrive.* MAUREEN *unpins the big blue rosette from her lapel.*

MAUREEN: What's up?
JULIA: We're waiting for the minister.
MAUREEN: How are you, Felix?
FELIX: All right.
MAUREEN: That's the way.
LYLE: Not a bad spot, this.
ASHLEIGH: Good place to be dead.
MAUREEN: Put a sock in it, you.

◆ ◆ ◆

NUGGET *and* LYLE *find themselves standing together, awkward in their best suits.*

LYLE: Nobby Taylor's sowing canola again.
NUGGET: He must have lost enough money on that by now. [*Pause.*] How's the hand?
LYLE: Fucked.
NUGGET: That's no good.
LYLE: [*good naturedly*] You'll keep, you bastard.

◆ ◆ ◆

FELIX: Last time I saw those two, they were laying into each other. Like really trying to injure the other person. I'd never seen that before.
ASHLEIGH: You don't get out much.

◆ ◆ ◆

LYLE: [*to* NUGGET] Yeah, all very well Nobby coming up with these schemes and showing us his computer spreadsheets, but if you get a year like this…
NUGGET: Nobby's old man'd be spewing.

◆ ◆ ◆

FELIX: What's with all the Nobbys and Dongers?
WILLIAM: Haven't you noticed? There's something of a theme in this town. Nobby Taylor, Donger Maloney, Horny McDonald.
JULIA: Horse Horrigan.
LYLE: He had a whopper.
WILLIAM: I'll say. I used to go down to the football shed just to have a look.
DIBS: Honestly, Will.
WILLIAM: His wife would walk down the street and all the locals'd say, 'Jeez, I wonder how she's managing Horse'.
DIBS: William, please.

They resume respectful silence. LYLE *can't resist.*

LYLE: Remember Doug Page?

JULIA: Pagey.

LYLE: I used to sit next to him at school. This one time I look across and there's Pagey writing his name on his dick. D. Page. Like kids write on the back of their ruler. I say to him, 'Jeez mate. It's not like anyone's gonna steal it.'

Everyone laughs.

GIRLIE: Lyle!

◆ ◆ ◆

MAUREEN *takes the opportunity for a private aside with* WILLIAM *and* JULIA. FELIX *eavesdrops.*

MAUREEN: I suggest that you two better move quickly. If you want a piece of the action.

JULIA: Maureen. Honestly. He's not even in the ground yet.

MAUREEN: Up to you. Just thought you should know. Nugget's been working on him pretty hard.

WILLIAM: What d'you mean?

MAUREEN: Farley won't have divided up the property.

JULIA: I understand that.

MAUREEN: No one in their right mind'd do that. Not even a mean old bastard like him.

JULIA: I think you'll find our father had a sense of fair play.

MAUREEN: Yeah. Standing by, while we scraped and struggled. Working like dogs—

WILLIAM: What's Nugget been doing?

MAUREEN: Well, he's the only farmer on your side of the family. And then there's the other business of course.

WILLIAM: What other business?

MAUREEN: I think you know.

WILLIAM: What are you talking about?

MAUREEN: Good grief. Is he fair dinkum?

WILLIAM: What are you on about?

MAUREEN: Nugget was born on the wrong side of the blanket. You know that, don't you?

JULIA: What?

MAUREEN: Your old man took advantage of a nineteen-year-old Aboriginal girl.

WILLIAM: Excuse me?

JULIA: What Aboriginal girl?

MAUREEN: You lot never cease to amaze me.

JULIA: Maureen. What Aboriginal girl?

MAUREEN: Joyce, her name was.

WILLIAM: This is bullshit.

JULIA: Joyce. That was her name. Nugget's mother.

WILLIAM: This is totally inappropriate.

MAUREEN: Sorry.

WILLIAM: Our father was a man of rigid morality.

MAUREEN: Ask Dibs.

JULIA: She would have told us.

MAUREEN: You were at boarding school.

WILLIAM: And you are a poisonous witch.

MAUREEN: Face it, you pompous git. Your father porked a gin. In the back room of our hotel. So don't give me any shit about what a principled man he was.

MAUREEN leaves.

GIRLIE: Maureen? [*To* JULIA] What's up with her?

Pause. She approaches JULIA.

We were expecting to meet your bloke.

JULIA: What?

GIRLIE: Your Indian gentleman.

JULIA: Oh. He couldn't come.

GIRLIE: That's a pity.

◆ ◆ ◆

FELIX *guides* JULIA *away from the group.*

FELIX: What happened to Nugget's mother?

JULIA: She was killed. In a car accident.

FELIX: Jesus. Does Grandma know about… you know… Grandpa and… Joyce?

JULIA: [*shrugging*] No. She can't. She wouldn't have taken Nugget on. Would she? If she knew?

FELIX: She's a Christian. They do all sorts of weird shit.

◆ ◆ ◆

LYLE: There's the minister. Over there.

LYLE *waves.*

WILLIAM: Thank Christ for that! Give us a hand, will you?

The men lift the coffin and the family exit, leaving behind NUGGET *and* FELIX.

◆ ◆ ◆

FELIX: Are you all right?

NUGGET: We were mates. [*Pause.*] We were real mates. [*Pause.*] He taught me how to kick the footy.

FELIX: I heard you were the most crap full forward Rushton's ever had.

NUGGET: We did all right. Won the flag three years on the trot. [*Pause.*] I hit him once, you know, after training.

FELIX: How come?

NUGGET: Dunno. He got me pretty riled-up though, so I slugged him. But he hit me back. Broke a couple of ribs.

FELIX: As you do.

NUGGET: Yeah.

FELIX: What happened with your mum?

NUGGET: She had a job at Girlie and Joe's pub.

FELIX: Behind the bar?

NUGGET: No, she was working as a house maid. Cleaning rooms an' that. She had a bookkeeping certificate, but there she was mopping up after all them piss-heads, down there.

FELIX: That'd be right.

NUGGET: One day I come home from school and there's Aunty Girl workin' behind the bar. She says to me, 'Go and watch telly. Joe's got something to tell you but he's not here yet.' So I go and watch TV and then Lucky Joe comes in and he says, 'Your mum's dead. She's been killed in a car accident on the Swan Hill Road. Be brave.' And then he just walks off.

FELIX: Shit. How old were you?

NUGGET: Ten. Next thing I know, Waxy Kirk's driving me up to Allandale. Farley and Dibs—they don't know what to say. So it's never mentioned again. Me mum… or me dad… never mentioned in that house.

FELIX: What is it with these people? [*Pause.*] Maureen reckons you're Farley's son.

Wayne Blair (left) as Nugget and Gareth Ellis as Felix in the 2003 Melbourne Theatre Company production. (Photo: Jeff Busby)

NUGGET: Does she?

FELIX: Is it true?

NUGGET: Oh, yeah. Farley's m'father. And Dibs is m'mother. That's how it's been since I was ten. Since they took me in. 'Cause they're the most Christian people you're ever likely to meet.

◆ ◆ ◆ ◆ ◆

SCENE FOUR

The Hamiltons'.

DIBS *and* JULIA *are sorting through Farley's wardrobe, throwing clothes on the bed.*

DIBS: Maybe Felix would like to have a look? There's a good navy suit in there.

JULIA: I don't think so.

DIBS: What about Lyle then?

JULIA: He doesn't want Dad's cast-offs.

DIBS: Don't be silly. They haven't got two pennies to rub together, that lot.

JULIA: Aren't you glad I didn't marry a farmer?

DIBS: I wish you'd stayed married to Hamish.

JULIA: Mum, Hamish is a homosexual.

DIBS: People do cope with all sorts of difficulties in marriage.

JULIA: He has sex with men.

DIBS: Maybe you just didn't try hard enough.

> JULIA *takes a deep breath.*

JULIA: Let's make this the bag for the Brotherhood, shall we? [*Pause.*] I was thinking about you last night. You really are quite extraordinary.

DIBS: How's that?

JULIA: Taking Nugget on. Under the circumstances. You have a remarkable capacity for forgiveness.

DIBS: Julia. Nugget was a little boy who didn't have a mother or a father.

JULIA: He had a father.

DIBS: Why don't we put all the shoes in here? You sure Felix wouldn't like these?

JULIA: He did have a father—

DIBS: They've hardly been worn, these shoes—

JULIA: —didn't he, Mum?

DIBS: Well, your Indian boyfriend obviously doesn't feel the need to take any responsibility.

JULIA: I'll manage.

DIBS: I don't know what you thought you were doing.

JULIA: I wanted a baby.

DIBS: So you just got yourself pregnant.

JULIA: I wanted a man as well as a baby, actually.

DIBS: Then why didn't you choose a proper man?

JULIA: He is a proper man.

DIBS: Don't throw that out. For heaven's sake. That's a new shirt. [*Pause.*] No one knows who Nugget's father was. Least of all the girl herself. Joyce.

JULIA: Maureen seems to know.

DIBS: People are full of gossip. Always have been.

> NUGGET *comes to the door.*

JULIA: Nuggs!

NUGGET: G'day. What's going on here?

DIBS: Just sorting through some things.

JULIA: Chucking out stuff.

NUGGET: Don't chuck out his hat, will you?

DIBS: No. We won't chuck out his hat.

NUGGET: Good.

> NUGGET *exits.*

JULIA: I've been talking to Nugget about my herb idea. He said I could use the seventy acres down at Burns's.

> *Pause.*

DIBS: The land is not Nugget's to give away.

JULIA: He's not giving it away. I'm your daughter.

DIBS: You've made your life in the city.

JULIA: I'm not going to settle for the pearl necklace, if that's what you're thinking.

DIBS: Julia, I'm not dead yet.

JULIA: I know, Mum, I just don't want you to rush in—

DIBS: Anyway, a farm like this has to be left intact.

JULIA: I am not suggesting we carve it up. I'm trying to find a way of keeping it in the family. We'd all be tenants in common: William and Nugget and me—

DIBS: Julia—

JULIA: —and you of course—

DIBS: —darling. You have a good job in the Multicultural Commission—

JULIA: —and I'm stressed out of my brain. My relationship has fallen in a heap and in two months time I'm going to have a little baby to look after. I want to change my life.

DIBS: You haven't thought this through.

JULIA: I have. I promise you. I have.

    Pause.

DIBS: I think I'll give these to Lyle and if he doesn't want them he can just say no. No harm done.

◆ ◆ ◆ ◆ ◆

LYLE *and* GIRLIE *enter their backyard.* GIRLIE *is attending to some washing. She holds up a pair of tattered footy shorts.*

GIRLIE: Can I turf these?

LYLE: No.

GIRLIE: What?

LYLE: No!

GIRLIE: All right. Keep your hair on.

◆ ◆ ◆ ◆ ◆

JULIA: Mum? I need to know what's happening?

DIBS: Perhaps we should talk to Will.

JULIA: William wants you to sell this place because he's scared of losing Kevin.

DIBS: What??

JULIA: That's what this boutique winery business is all about. It's Kevin's project. Not William's. Will doesn't know anything about grapes.

DIBS: I know.

JULIA: William is a restaurateur.

DIBS: That's what I said to him. I said, 'You don't know anything about grapes'.

JULIA: But what Kevin wants, Kevin gets. And quite frankly, Mum, the idea that we might sell Allandale—our family farm—to make Kevin happy. Hello?! [*Beat.*] William is not very secure, you know. In himself. And sometimes people like that can be easily corrupted.

DIBS: Julia. He's your brother.

JULIA: So is Nugget. Mum?

> *Pause.*

DIBS: He was a good man, your father. Don't sling mud at him now.

> DIBS *exits.*

◆ ◆ ◆ ◆ ◆

SCENE FIVE

The Delaneys' backyard.

BRIANNA *is helping* GIRLIE *hang out the washing.* LYLE *is plaiting a whip and listening to the races on the radio.* MAUREEN *and* ASHLEIGH *enter.* MAUREEN *has a package of election posters.*

MAUREEN: What's this?

ASHLEIGH: Benalla. Race eight.

MAUREEN: Saw Father Kelly up the shops. I asked him what he was going to do at the concert and he reckons he might whistle 'Ramona'.

She whistles the tune.

BRIANNA: He did that last year.

LYLE: Shut up, will ya?

MAUREEN: And the year before. Silly coot.

ASHLEIGH: Do I have to go?

LYLE: Of course you bloody-well have to go!

MAUREEN: What's up with him?

LYLE: I'm listening to the bloody race!

MAUREEN: Lyle!

GIRLIE *switches it off.*

GIRLIE: Are you gonna tell her or am I? [*Pause.*] We've had a visit from the bailiff.

MAUREEN: What?

GIRLIE: The bank's served us with an eviction notice.

MAUREEN: Bullshit.

LYLE *grabs the transistor and exits.*

Lyle? What's happening? Lyle?

GIRLIE: Remember the three-tonne seeder he bought off Jack Cummins?

BRIANNA: And the tractor.

GIRLIE: He put up the house as security.

MAUREEN: What a useless idiot.

GIRLIE: Nugget said he'd go in halves apparently. With the seeder. But then he backed out. That's what that fight was about.

MAUREEN: I'm married to a hopeless piece of trash.

GIRLIE: He's doing his best.

MAUREEN: Fat lot of good, that is.

ASHLEIGH: Will we have to go on the dole?

MAUREEN *storms to the doorway and yells out:*

MAUREEN: [*screaming off*] You hopeless bloody loser!

GIRLIE: What are we gonna do, Mor?

MAUREEN: We're gonna claim what's ours. That's what we're gonna do.

◆ ◆ ◆ ◆ ◆

SCENE SIX

The Hamiltons' bedroom.

DIBS *enters to find* WILLIAM *rifling through his father's writing desk.*

DIBS: What are you doing?

WILLIAM: I'm looking for the will.

DIBS: It's with the solicitor.

WILLIAM: Uh-huh.

DIBS: We made one about ten years ago.

WILLIAM: Mm-hmm.

DIBS: I can tell you what's in it.

> WILLIAM *seizes upon an envelope. He opens it deftly with a letter opener.*

William! Please!

> WILLIAM *examines the contents carefully.*

Monica Maughan as Dibs and Rhys McConnochie as William in the 2003 Melbourne Theatre Company production. (Photo: Jeff Busby)

WILLIAM: [*reading*] 'I hereby revoke all former Wills and testamentary dispositions (made by me) and declare this to be my last Will and Testament.'

He turns the pages to note the date and the witnesses.

[*Reading*] 'Dated this day Monday 26th April 1999. Witnessed by Frederick Barnard and Frank Scott.' [*Pause.*] Who are they? Mum?

DIBS: [*quietly*] Airforce chums. Bunty Barnard and Wing-Commander Scott.

WILLIAM: He must have gone down to Melbourne. Did you know about this?

DIBS: Must have been Anzac Day.

WILLIAM: [*reading*] 'After payment of my just debts, testamentary and funeral expenses and any taxes or duties payable as a result of my death, I give my entire remaining estate to my son Neville Hamilton, known as Nugget.'

DIBS: Let me look at that.

WILLIAM: [*reading*] 'I do hereby devise and bequeath the old house block… matrimonial home and garden… motor vehicle… money held in my name… Commonwealth Bank, Swan Hill, to my spouse Elizabeth Hamilton, known as Dibs.'

DIBS: Give me that.

WILLIAM: My son, Neville Hamilton. Known as Nugget.

Silence.

What are we to understand from this?

DIBS: He didn't have anywhere else to go. So we adopted him.

WILLIAM: But who's his father. Who is Nugget's father?

DIBS: Unknown. It says 'Unknown' on his birth certificate. Give me that.

WILLIAM *hands her the will.* DIBS *rips it up.*

This is not Farley's farm. This is my farm. And I will decide how it's to be operated from now on. No one gets anything until I say so.

NUGGET *enters.*

WILLIAM: Haven't you heard of knocking?

NUGGET: What?

WILLIAM: Knock before you come in.

NUGGET: Get real.

DIBS: What is it, Nugget?

WILLIAM: Did you want something?

Pause.

NUGGET: Farley reckoned there was something in his desk.

WILLIAM: What sort of something?

NUGGET: None of your business.

WILLIAM: If my father said there was something in his desk for you, then I'd like to know what it is.

NUGGET: It wasn't for you, mate. It was for me.

WILLIAM: What is it?

Pause.

NUGGET: His will.

WILLIAM: His will is with the solicitors in Swan Hill.

NUGGET: It's in the third drawer.

WILLIAM: Take a look.

WILLIAM *and* NUGGET *stare at each other.*

NUGGET: Farley left me the farm.

DIBS: We've done everything we can for you, Nugget.

NUGGET: He left it to me.

DIBS: You don't seem very grateful for what we've done.

NUGGET: Grateful?

WILLIAM: Yes.

NUGGET: Grateful.

WILLIAM: Frankly, this fantasy you've dreamt up—I find it quite an affront. I mean, who do you think you are?

NUGGET: Farley's son.

WILLIAM: That's a lie. Your father was a rabbito.

NUGGET: That's bullshit, mate.

WILLIAM: You conniving little cheat.

NUGGET: I'm not taking the farm off you.

WILLIAM: You're dead right, you're not.

NUGGET: I'm keeping it in the family.

DIBS: You're not family. I'm sorry. But you're not.

> WILLIAM *pulls the drawer out to show* NUGGET.

WILLIAM: There's nothing in here for you.

> NUGGET *exits, slamming the door behind him.*

DIBS: He's not family. He's not.

◆ ◆ ◆ ◆ ◆

SCENE SEVEN

FELIX *is reading a book in the kitchen.* JULIA *enters.*

JULIA: So, my father has joined a long line of farmers who've exploited Aboriginal women. That's great, isn't it? Just another white man who couldn't keep his dick in his trousers.

FELIX: Maybe he loved her.

JULIA: Maybe he did. Maybe he really loved her. Why did I make that assumption—automatically—that it was exploitative?

FELIX: Because she was nineteen.

JULIA: That's right. She was nineteen. And how old was he?

FELIX: I don't know. Forty something.

JULIA: See, that sucks.

FELIX: I can't imagine any woman wanting to… be nice to him even, let alone—you know—have sex with him.

JULIA: Oh, God. Poor Mum… poor Mum.

> *She sees* NUGGET *walk past outside. He's agitated.*

[*Calling*] Nuggs! Nugget!

> WILLIAM *enters.*

What's wrong with Nugget?

WILLIAM: He's adjourned to the shed. His grief is more intense than ours.

JULIA: Will!

FELIX: That is so fucked!

JULIA: How would you feel if you weren't allowed to acknowledge your own father?

WILLIAM: Now look. I want you both to understand this very clearly. Dad is not Nugget's father. And it would be reprehensible if you indulged in some leftie guilt trip—

JULIA: You are in such denial.

WILLIAM: Our father did not touch that girl.

FELIX: Joyce.

JULIA: How can you be so sure?

WILLIAM: This is our father we're talking about.

JULIA: You hate him. You've hated Dad all your life.

WILLIAM: That still doesn't give me the right to call him a rapist—

FELIX: No one's accusing him of rape.

WILLIAM: Shut up, Felix, for chrissake!

FELIX: No. Get fucked. I won't.

From left: Jody Kennedy as Brianna, Katherine Fyffe as Ashleigh and Steve Bisley as Lyle in the 2003 Melbourne Theatre Company production. (Photo: Jeff Busby)

DIBS: [*offstage, to the dogs*] Blackie! Mack! Shut up!

FELIX: You're just worried about your vineyard.

WILLIAM: Oh, really.

FELIX: You're up shit creek, aren't you? You can't just con Nanna Dibs into selling this place. Not now—

DIBS: [*offstage, to the dogs*] Get out, Mack!

FELIX: —now that Nugget's got a claim on the farm.

WILLIAM: Nugget has no claim on this farm. You are such a gullible little bleeding heart. You'd believe anything.

> DIBS *enters.*

DIBS: Dinner's ready.

WILLIAM: Can I give you a hand, Mum?

DIBS: No, I'm right thanks. Now this is beef and vegetables. Felix, you'll have to pick out the beef.

WILLIAM: Don't tell me you're still a vegetarian.

DIBS: That's why he's so pale.

JULIA: It'd be good if you could be a little less judgmental.

WILLIAM: Why?

JULIA: You sound just like Dad.

DIBS: Ssh, ssh, ssh. Enough. Goodness me. Would you say grace, William?

WILLIAM: For what we are about to receive, may the Lord make us truly thankful. Amen.

> *A full chorus of 'Praise My Soul, the King of Heaven'. The sound of tyres and dogs.*

◆ ◆ ◆ ◆ ◆

SCENE EIGHT

The back doors roll open and the Delaneys' ute, piled high with their belongings, rolls down the stage towards the audience.

The truck comes to a stop and LYLE *climbs down. The others wait in the car. The Hamiltons are gathered to meet them.*

LYLE: Sorry about this, Auntie Dibs. Jules. Will. Felix. We've come to give you a hand. [*Pause.*] Since Farley's... passed away, you're gonna need a farmer. I'd be willing to help you out.

CHOIR: [*singing*]
　　　　Praise Him! Praise Him! Praise the everlasting King!

◆ ◆ ◆ ◆ ◆

SCENE NINE

In the kitchen.

WILLIAM: This is preposterous. What do they think they're doing?

DIBS: They've been evicted.

WILLIAM: So?

DIBS: They've got nowhere else to go.

WILLIAM: That is not our problem.

DIBS: She is my sister. Show some compassion.

WILLIAM: You can't agree to this.

　　　　ASHLEIGH *enters carrying a birdcage with a budgie in it.*

ASHLEIGH: Where do you want me to put Frank?

WILLIAM: In the shed.

DIBS: Give him to me, Ash.

ASHLEIGH: Nanna said to keep him in the kitchen.

DIBS: We'll put him here for the time being. Do you think he'll be happy here?

ASHLEIGH: I don't think so.

　　　　ASHLEIGH *exits.*

WILLIAM: Very sullen little Miss, that one.

DIBS: Would you turn your sister away if she came to you, in need?

WILLIAM: My sister is not trying to take over my estate.

DIBS: What sort of a man are you, William? Is this what your lifestyle has given rise to?

WILLIAM: What are you implying, Mother?

DIBS: You don't seem to understand what it must be like to have to pack your things onto a truck and put yourself at the mercy of someone else.

WILLIAM: I would never be in that position. I make choices. I set goals and then I take action to achieve them.

DIBS: You eat, you drink, you travel, you furnish your house with expensive things. You never have to put yourself out for anyone.

WILLIAM: I work hard for the money I earn. These people are parasites.

DIBS: These people are your family.

WILLIAM: Kevin is my family.

DIBS: You don't have children. That's the difference. You don't know what it means to put yourself second. And as a result you seem to have lost the capacity for human charity.

FELIX *enters.*

FELIX: Nan?

DIBS: What, love?

FELIX: We seem to have a mouse plague.

There is screaming from the back of the house.

They're eating the putty out of the shed windows.

DIBS: It's these mild winters. They get out of hand.

WILLIAM *goes to the window.*

WILLIAM: Bloody hell! Look at that!

FELIX: That pile of grain. It's moving!

FELIX *shudders with revulsion. Suddenly he screams, beating his trouser leg.*

Jesus! What was that?

He screams again.

DIBS: Oh, for goodness sake, you ridiculous child.

FELIX *reaches inside his trouser leg and throws out a mouse.* DIBS *stomps on it.*

Get a grip on yourself! You really are quite pathetic.

DIBS *exits.*

◆ ◆ ◆ ◆ ◆

SCENE TEN

Farley's bedroom.

BRIANNA *is unpacking and* LYLE *is plugging holes to prevent mice getting in.* ASHLEIGH *bursts in.*

ASHLEIGH: I hate this place. I hate it. I hate it. I hate it.
LYLE: Settle down, for chrissake.
ASHLEIGH: The worst thing is having to be here with that poofter.
LYLE: Hey! Enough!
ASHLEIGH: Why did you make us come here? It's not fair.
LYLE: Life is not fair. Get that into your thick head.
ASHLEIGH: I am supposed to be at Teaghan Kelly's birthday party.
LYLE: Boo hoo.
BRIANNA: You said you didn't want to go.
ASHLEIGH: Yeah, well it's totally humiliating. I just hope that no one finds out.
BRIANNA: Ashleigh.
ASHLEIGH: Even a baby knows you don't borrow money when you're like up to your eyeballs in debt.
BRIANNA: Ash.
ASHLEIGH: It's all his fault. He's such a fucking loser.

> LYLE *rushes forward about to slap her hard across the face, but he checks himself in time. He exits.*

◆ ◆ ◆ ◆ ◆

SCENE ELEVEN

The kitchen.

The legs of the table have been stood in ice cream containers. FELIX *is filling them with water.* JULIA *is on the phone.*

JULIA: [*into the phone*] Come on, Nugget, pick up.

FELIX: Is he there?

JULIA: [*hanging up*] No.

FELIX: Where's Annie living these days?

JULIA: Horsham, I think. I don't have a number for her.

> LYLE *walks hastily through the room.*

Lyle? Have you seen Nugget around?

LYLE: Nup.

JULIA: Is his ute here?

LYLE: Dunno.

JULIA: What happened between you two, Lyle?

LYLE: What d'you mean?

JULIA: You used to be mates.

LYLE: People change, don't they?

JULIA: Do they?

LYLE: He started to get a bit big for his boots, ol' Nugget. Gave me the shits. Not just me. Lots of blokes round here felt the same. He's a good worker, Nugget. Trouble is, he's got big ideas.

JULIA: What's wrong with that?

LYLE: If you don't know, I can't explain it to you.

FELIX: You can't explain it because you know it sounds ugly.

JULIA: Felix.

FELIX: At the end of the day, you can't accept that an Aborigine'd have ideas.

LYLE: Listen, city boy—you don't have to live with them. You don't know what it's like. And I can tell you, it's not all rainbow serpents and sacred sites.

JULIA: Lyle, we're talking about Nugget. My brother Nugget.

LYLE: Yeah, well he seems to have gone walkabout. And if he never comes back, that'll be too soon.

> LYLE *exits.*

FELIX: We live in a ghetto, Mum. We all think the same, but out here— they hate blacks, they hate wogs. They hate brown people.

JULIA: Not all of them are like that.

FELIX: Name one.

JULIA: Mum. She raised Nugget. She loves him.

> MAUREEN *enters.*

MAUREEN: I'm looking for a little brown suitcase. Have you seen it?

FELIX: I think I might head back tomorrow, Mum. Now the asylum seekers have moved in.

MAUREEN: You're a very arrogant young man, aren't you?

FELIX: I have a very low tolerance for hypocrisy.

MAUREEN: Meaning?

FELIX: Meaning that I couldn't possibly be pleasant to you, since your politics are so obnoxious.

MAUREEN: You're stupid as well as rude.

JULIA: How long are you planning to be here, Maureen?

MAUREEN: We're more hospitable in the bush, Julia. But I was going to ask you the same question. When are you heading back?

JULIA: I haven't decided yet.

MAUREEN: It's all the same to me. You can stay as long as you like, as far as I'm concerned.

JULIA: Excuse me?

FELIX: I hope that the people round here don't fall for your racism and prejudice.

MAUREEN: Listen. There is nothing racist about my policies. That's why you're so dumb. You can't see. I've spent every day this past year— telling the people out there that Aboriginals are just the same as what we are.

FELIX: You don't believe that.

MAUREEN: Bullshit. They're just as Australian. And they deserve just the same respect as any white person. It's just the extra privileges they get which make people round here mad.

FELIX: Is that why you campaigned against Nugget being appointed to the Mallee Catchment Authority?

MAUREEN: Who told you that?

FELIX: Why do you tell people that he's not much of a farmer?

MAUREEN: Where do you get this stuff from?

FELIX: It's either racism or self-interest. Which one is it?

MAUREEN: You just make it up, don't you, to discredit people like me, who are actually trying to stand up for Australia? Because you're from the city, you think you know everything. It's a big joke out this way. You're so politically correct, you wouldn't know your arse from your armpit. I'd shut up and learn a few things first, if I were you, buddy boy.

◆ ◆ ◆ ◆ ◆

SCENE TWELVE

Night is falling. Dogs howl and yelp at the mice. In the kitchen, DIBS *makes herself a cup of tea. Suddenly it is all too much. She leans on the table and starts to sob.* GIRLIE *appears.*

GIRLIE: Come on, you.

DIBS: Sorry. [*Pause.*] I don't usually go to pieces.

GIRLIE: Doesn't hurt to have a good howl.

> *Pause.*

DIBS: I've done something terrible. [*Pause.*] Farley changed his will. William found it this morning. [*Pause.*] He left the farm to Nugget.

GIRLIE: He can't do that.

DIBS: I tore it up.

GIRLIE: Good. You've given him every opportunity, that kid.

DIBS: I don't know what more we could have done.

GIRLIE: Nothing.

DIBS: Farley made that will the day after Anzac Day, couple of years ago.

GIRLIE: Oh, that settles it then. He was tanked to the eyeballs. It's not the act of a rational man.

DIBS: What sort of a marriage is it where a husband'd change his will and not tell his wife?

> *Pause.*

GIRLIE: Tell you what. Why don't you and me nick off for a couple of days? Leave them to it. It'd do you good, Dibble.

DIBS: I can't.

GIRLIE: Yes, you can.

DIBS: Where would we go?

GIRLIE: What about the Grand?

DIBS: In Mildura? Don't be ridiculous. That'd cost a fortune.

GIRLIE: Not for us, it wouldn't. Remember that raffle I won at St Joey's? Two nights at the Grand Hotel. All expenses paid.

DIBS: That was about two years ago.

GIRLIE: So? I've been waiting for me chance. Come on, Dibble. You deserve a break. You've suffered enough.

DIBS: This is not about me. This is about the farm. Oh, dear. What's going to happen to Nugget now?

GIRLIE: Why ever did you take him on? I never understood. She had family, Joyce did.

DIBS: They couldn't look after him like we could. He had a proper home here and proper schooling.

GIRLIE: Was it your idea or Farley's?

DIBS: We all do the wrong thing from time to time.

GIRLIE: Mmm.

DIBS: He wasn't proud of himself, Farley—if that's what you're thinking.

GIRLIE: No.

DIBS: And Nugget being here with us—it was a daily reminder of his own weakness. His own shame.

GIRLIE: So whose idea was it?

DIBS: Mine. But I'm buggered if I'm going to honour his bloody dying wishes. I kept Farley's secret for thirty-eight years, Girl. I stood by him all that time—and then he goes and does this. He expects me to hand over my family farm to his bastard son. What sort of a man does that? I am not giving Nugget a single handful of this dirt.

◆ ◆ ◆ ◆ ◆

SCENE THIRTEEN

NUGGET *sits on a fence in the middle of the farm. He places Farley's hat on the post next to him. As he begins to speak,* FARLEY *appears.*

NUGGET: I come home from school one day with a black eye. Remember? And you go, 'Right, come out here'.

FARLEY *puts on his hat.*

FARLEY: A kid like you needs to know how to defend himself.

NUGGET: A kid like me?

FARLEY: Come on, come on, keep your guard up, keep your guard up—throw your punch—good.

NUGGET: I remember lying in bed that night thinking, 'What do you mean? A kid like me?'

FARLEY: Harder. Come in harder.

NUGGET: Most of the time you used to say, 'You're no different to anyone else in this family'.

FARLEY: 'No better and no worse.' Go in with your elbow. In hard. Go on. That's it.

NUGGET: But I'd see blackfellas in the street up in Swan Hill. I knew they were watching us. They'd give me a smile, but they were too shy, you know. They were thinking—he's with them now.

FARLEY: I never thought of you as a blackfella.

NUGGET: Well, you must have been blind.

FARLEY: I didn't want you getting mixed up with them—

NUGGET: —because you were scared they'd tell me the truth. [*Pause.*] Why couldn't you just tell me.

FARLEY: I always treated you like a son.

NUGGET: That's not enough.

FARLEY: What more did you want?

NUGGET: I'm up shit creek. Can't you see, you silly old bastard? This is my country. This should be my farm. But they've pulled the fucking rug from under me. I haven't got a leg to stand on. Because you wouldn't say I had a right to it. Because you wouldn't tell them the truth.

FARLEY: Some things are best left unsaid, mate.

◆ ◆ ◆ ◆ ◆

SCENE FOURTEEN

LYLE *drives his ute into a lonely paddock. His expensive, powerful car stereo is blaring Country and Western music into the night.* LYLE *gets out of the ute with a six-pack—and an open can in his hand. He is drunk. He shuts off the music. Silence. He drinks. Silence.*

LYLE: [*to the audience*] What are you fucking looking at? What? Baa-aaa-aa. Baaaaaaaaa. Two, four, ten, fifty, two thousand. Two thousand stupid, useless bags of chops.

He reaches into the ute and gets his rifle.

When they take you outta here, when Waxy drives you off in his semi, it's off to the fucking meatworks for you. You're dead meat!

He mimics taking pot shots into the audience.

Bang. Bang. Bang. Fucking bang.

He puts down the rifle. Drinks.

Sunday bloody roast.

He powers up an imaginary chainsaw and starts to carve up his own body.

Bzzzzzz. Ribs. Bzzzzzz. Chops. Bzzzzzz. Lamb's fucking fry.

He bangs his head with the heel of his palm—violently.

No fucking brains. No fucking brains, Lyle Delaney. No fucking brains. They'll put you on the chopping board: fucking bank manager, fucking bailiff, Maureen Bloody Lend-A-Hand Delaney. They'll bloody mince you in the big fucking mincer.

He goes on drinking.

'Get big or get out.' Get big, fat and hard. Or bloody flop out of your farm. So there I am pulling myself for all I'm worth—big header, big car, big ideas, big mortgage. One big, dumb ram with his fucking knackers dragging on the ground.

Oh, God, I'm fucked.

What's a farmer without a farm? Ay? Ay? A bloody grunt. A bloody odd-job man with no fancy-nancy certificates, no diploma, no shiny-arsed qualifications. A fucking refugee. Fucking nothing.

Oh, Christ. Look at this place. Look at this fucking, dry twat of a place.

He's down in the dirt.

I've bloody dug it, ploughed it, shat on it, fucked it. I love this—I love this place. And I'm not going to fucking die in the dole queue. Get butchered by bloody Centrelink. A man has to live or die on his own piece of dirt. That's always been the way, hasn't it?

He takes another long swig from the bottle.

Look at me when I'm bloody talking to you. Look—at—me!

He takes the rifle and fires it into the night.

Blackout.

◆ ◆ ◆ ◆ ◆

SCENE FIFTEEN

The Grand Hotel, Mildura.

DIBS *and* GIRLIE *are in their best clothes sitting at a table, sipping wine and perusing the menu.*

GIRLIE: This is the life, eh Sis?

DIBS: Don't mind if I do, Girl.

GIRLIE: Thought this place'd be full of snoots.

DIBS: We brush up all right, in this company. If I do say so myself.

GIRLIE: Not a bad drop, this chardonnay.

DIBS: They're the grapes William wants to grow. On the Peninsula.

GIRLIE: What's happened about that?

DIBS: I would not throw in my lot with that boy, for love nor money.

GIRLIE: You've changed your tune.

DIBS: Oh, Girl. I'm too old. And if I told you the God-honest truth—I don't really like him that much.

> GIRLIE *snorts.*

It's dreadful, isn't it? Whoever heard a mother say that? I thought for a while that I should make up somehow. That he deserved something from us.

GIRLIE: How d'you mean?

DIBS: He always acts like I owe him. Because he had such a hard time with Farley.

GIRLIE: How old is he?

DIBS: Fifty-two.

GIRLIE: I think it's time he got over it. [*Pause. Referring to the menu*] You don't think we'll have to eat pigeon, do you? I couldn't. I couldn't do that to Lyle.

DIBS: Julia says it's very nice.

GIRLIE: She's making that boy of hers a bloody wuss, isn't she?

DIBS: Shocking.

GIRLIE: What's the matter with her? If ever there was a kid that needed to develop a bit of muscle.

DIBS: He's a vegan, apparently.

GIRLIE: What? From Venus?

◆ ◆ ◆ ◆ ◆

SCENE SIXTEEN

The Hamiltons' woolshed.

FELIX *is alone, smoking a joint.* BRIANNA *opens the door.*

BRIANNA: Hey.

FELIX: Hey.

BRIANNA: I was looking for Ashleigh.

FELIX: Sorry.

BRIANNA: Have you ever seen one of these? [*She opens her hand to reveal an axe head.*] It's an Aboriginal axe head.

FELIX: Cool.

BRIANNA: Nugget and me found it down at Burns's.

FELIX: They've shafted him, you know.

BRIANNA: Who has?

FELIX: The family. Nanna Dibs. He won't get the farm now.

BRIANNA: Who is getting it?

> FELIX *shrugs.*

If she sells up, that'll be the end of us. We'll have to move.

FELIX: This is Nugget's country. His people have already been dispossessed once. He has a spiritual attachment to this place.

BRIANNA: I know, but so do we.

FELIX: How can you say that?

BRIANNA: You don't like it up here, so you don't understand. But to Dad… and me… Dad could tell you every tree, every hill. Every creek. We belong here too.

FELIX: Nugget told me once. He said, 'I don't need to own it, mate. That's the difference between us blackfellas and your mob.' But the truth is, Brianna, if you don't own it—if your name isn't on the title—they'll shaft you.

> *Pause.*

BRIANNA: It's like whatever decision Dad makes, it doesn't work out. But it's not his fault. Yesterday I saw him in the pigeon loft and he was crying. He lost his best bird last week—Little Red. She just didn't come home. He's beside himself, worrying about that bird—Mum doesn't understand any of this—and then last night he said, 'Maybe she doesn't want to come home. Why would a beautiful bird like Little Red waste her time hanging out with me?'

> *She starts to cry.* FELIX *puts his arms around her. Suddenly the shed door is flung open and* LYLE *stands in the shadows, carrying a whip. He strides towards* FELIX, *shaking with drunken rage.*

LYLE: Get your filthy hands off her.

BRIANNA: Dad!

> LYLE *cracks the whip. The noise rips through the air.*

FELIX: Jesus Christ.

LYLE: Come here, you little runt.

> *He grabs* FELIX *and throws him to the ground.*

You keep your hands off my daughter.

BRIANNA: Dad! Daddy!

FELIX: Fuck, man. I didn't do—

> LYLE *whips* FELIX. BRIANNA *screams and rushes out to the house.*

LYLE: That'll teach ya. You weak little git.

> LYLE *whips him again and again.*

[*Panting for breath*] Don't you ever touch my daughter again.

> MAUREEN *enters and fires a gunshot.* LYLE *stops.*

MAUREEN: Give me that.

LYLE: Why don't you just shoot me?

MAUREEN: Give me that.

> LYLE *throws the whip on the ground.*

Get in the car. And don't come back.

> LYLE *slinks away into the night.* FELIX *whimpers. Blood is gushing from his face.*

You'll be right, mate. Come inside.

FELIX: Can you get my mum?

MAUREEN: [*seeing his face*] Christ.

> JULIA *enters and rushes over to* FELIX.

JULIA: Felix! What happened? Oh, my God. Child. What happened?

FELIX: He whipped me.

JULIA: Who whipped you? Felix? Who did this?

FELIX: Lyle.

MAUREEN: Let's get him inside. Come on.

JULIA: He needs a doctor.

MAUREEN: There is no doctor.

JULIA: What are you talking about? Where's the doctor?

MAUREEN: We don't have a doctor anymore.

FELIX: Jesus Christ. Help me.

◆ ◆ ◆ ◆ ◆

SCENE SEVENTEEN

The Grand Hotel, Mildura.

DIBS: Here's to us. Eighty years old and still going strong.

GIRLIE: Your children are doin' just fine. You've done a real good job on 'em. Don't you tell yourself otherwise.

DIBS: Thanks, Girl. You too. Well done.

GIRLIE: Lyle's the one who needs a leg up. He's a good boy, that one.

DIBS: I'll say.

GIRLIE: He's the one Wormie McCallum had pegged as the farmer in the family. Remember. On the day he was born, Wormie said, 'There's your farmer, Girl'.

DIBS: Why'd he say that?

GIRLIE: He was born just on harvest, three weeks premature. And you know what they say—that's the difference between a good farmer and a bad one. Three weeks. All in the timing.

DIBS: He was a dear little kid, your Lyle.

GIRLIE: His heart's in the right place. And he loves his Aunty Dibs. Always has.

DIBS: I got a soft spot for him.

GIRLIE: He just needs a little help from Lady Luck. For once in his life.

◆ ◆ ◆ ◆ ◆

SCENE EIGHTEEN

The Hamiltons'.

Next afternoon. WILLIAM *is playing the piano.* JULIA *enters.*

WILLIAM: Julia! How is he?

JULIA: He's a mess.

WILLIAM: Here. Sit down.

JULIA: No. I'm not staying. I can't trust myself. I'm just getting my stuff.

WILLIAM: Can I do anything?

JULIA: I've never hated anyone as much as I hate that animal and if I saw him now I'd go at him with a knife.

WILLIAM: He's not here.

JULIA: Just as well.

WILLIAM: Julia. Tell me about Felix.

JULIA: He hasn't spoken since it happened.

WILLIAM: How's his face?

JULIA: Fourteen stitches.

> ASHLEIGH *enters breathlessly. She has run all the way from the farm gate. She is wearing her blue school uniform.*

ASHLEIGH: Mum? Mum? Shit. Where is she? Bri?

JULIA: What's the matter, Ash?

ASHLEIGH: Where's Mum?

BRIANNA: She's in Warracknabeal.

ASHLEIGH: Oh, no!

BRIANNA: What's up? Ash, what's the matter?

ASHLEIGH: You know how the bank said they were gonna repossess our tractor?

BRIANNA: Yeah.

ASHLEIGH: I was sitting in the bus, just after school and some kid goes 'Look' and I look up and there's Dad driving the tractor down Campbell Street, at full pelt. And he's going, 'You want the tractor. I'll give you the fucking tractor.' And then he swings it around and drives it straight at the bank. Straight through the plate glass windows.

> *We hear the almighty crash of glass.*

BRIANNA: Is he all right?

> ASHLEIGH *shrugs.*

WILLIAM: Is anyone hurt?

ASHLEIGH: He's off his face. They should lock him up.

JULIA: Where is he, Ash?

ASHLEIGH: I don't know. I just stayed on the bus.

JULIA: I'm sorry, but I'm going to make sure that they lock him up.

◆ ◆ ◆ ◆ ◆

SCENE NINETEEN

Main Street, Mildura.

DIBS *comes running toward* GIRLIE *waving a piece of paper.*

DIBS: I've done it. Girl! Here—look. All legal and proper. See? I've transferred the property to Lyle.

GIRLIE: Oh, Dibs.

> *She hugs her.*

Good on you, love.

DIBS: See? Lyle Delaney.

GIRLIE: This is the best thing that's ever happened.

DIBS: He's the new owner of Allandale. We did it!

GIRLIE: This'll be the making of him. You see.

DIBS: We've kept it in the family.

GIRLIE: You've done the right thing.

DIBS: Anything else would have caused too many divisions.

GIRLIE: What did the solicitor say?

DIBS: He said it's always better to make clear decisions while you're alive, rather than have your children fight over it when you're gone.

GIRLIE: That's right.

DIBS: Better to hate me, than hate each other.

GIRLIE: Grandma Jessie would have approved.

DIBS: We'll have a toast to Jessie tonight, eh? After we've told everyone.

GIRLIE: Let's go, eh? I can't wait to tell 'em. This is the best thing that's happened to our family for as long as I can remember.

◆ ◆ ◆ ◆ ◆

SCENE TWENTY

The two girls in their blue school uniforms push open the big doors of the woolshed. LYLE *is hanging from the rafters.*

We hear DIBS *and* GIRLIE *singing 'Two Little Girls In Blue' as they drive along the highway towards Allandale, their voices brimming with happiness and hilarity.*

END OF ACT TWO

EPILOGUE

Melbourne. Julia's house. One year later.

JULIA *(nursing her baby),* FELIX *and* NUGGET *are watching the Federal Election on TV.*

A POLITICAL COMMENTATOR *is presenting the results with an* ELECTORAL STATISTICIAN.

COMMENTATOR: We've got more results in from the seat of Murray. Roly Piggot has held this seat for the Nationals for twenty-two years.

STATISTICIAN: There's a swing away from him of twelve percent. It's fallen into the hands of the new Independent candidate, Maureen Delaney.

COMMENTATOR: Should we count that as one for the Coalition? Or one for the ALP?

STATISTICIAN: Maureen Delaney's a wild card. If she ends up holding the balance of power, it'll make her the most powerful woman in the country.

COMMENTATOR: We can cross to Maureen Delaney's campaign headquarters in Swan Hill. Maureen Delaney, can you hear me?

MAUREEN: I hear you loud and clear, [*commentator's name*], and the voters of the Mallee are sending a loud and clear message to the whole of Australia. They're pioneers in this country and tonight they've pioneered a new path for Australian politics. They're putting Australia first and lending a hand.

COMMENTATOR: So, Maureen, you'll be talking to the leaders of both the principal parties?

MAUREEN: No, [*commentator's name*], they'll be talking to me.

COMMENTATOR: Now we've all heard the reports that you've had to sell the family farm to finance the campaign. Was that a hard decision?

MAUREEN: Well, [*commentator's name*], Allandale has been in our family for five generations. So of course it was a hard decision. But who wouldn't sell their farm to save their country?

An almighty cheer erupts from the crowd. They sing the campaign song 'Lend A Hand' boisterously.

NUGGET: Turn it off, will you?

FELIX *clicks the remote control.*

Blackout.

THE END

APPENDIX

'LEND A HAND'

Music and lyrics by Ian McDonald and Michael Cathcart.

Send out a warning
There's trouble in the land
Australia is calling
C'mon lend a hand
I'm trav'llin' on the highway
'Cause my heart is in the land
I'm headin' for the Mallee
Where I can lend a hand
Our future will be grand
Stand up for Australia
C'mon lend a hand
Lend a hand
It's time to take a stand
Australia is calling
C'mon lend a hand.

Music available from Ian McDonald, 50 Athelstan Road,
Camberwell, Vic., 3124, Australia.

◆ ◆ ◆ ◆ ◆

ALSO BY HANNIE RAYSON & AVAILABLE FROM CURRENCY PRESS

COMPETITIVE TENDERNESS

Dawn Snow has a fierce reputation—she reformed the prison system in Uganda. Now, with local government reform high on the political agenda, she is called upon to perform a similar task within the city of Greater Burke. *Competitive Tenderness* is topical, satirical and even a little anarchic, but most of all it is very, very funny indeed. Hannie Rayson's inspired farce takes a swipe at bureaucracy, corruption, romance and just about anything else that comes her way.

2 Acts—4M, 4W

0 86819 460 3

FALLING FROM GRACE

Falling From Grace is a play with a bright comic surface and mysterious depths. It is about women in medicine, in the media and in the office—power and authority in female hands. It is also about public morality and a struggle between women to see who should be its guardian. These women are best friends in a professional world. They are witty and erudite, passionate in their pursuit of success and relentless in their pursuit of passion. They juggle careers, children and lovers. They are forty and their friendship is about to be tested.

2 Acts—2M, 5W

086819 387 9

HOTEL SORRENTO

Hilary lives in seaside Sorrento with her father and sixteen-year-old son; Pippa is visiting from New York and Meg returns from England with her English husband. Three sisters, reunited after ten years in different worlds, again feel the constraints of family life. It is Meg's semi-autobiographical novel, recently short-listed for the Booker prize, which overshadows their homecoming.

'*Hotel Sorrento* is a powerful new Australian play that begins as a comedy about national identity and develops into a familial drama of great poignancy and reverberation.' Peter Craven—*Australian*

2 Acts—4M, 4W

0 86819 681 9

LIFE AFTER GEORGE

The play that broke box office records during its Melbourne premiere season. Peter George, charismatic academic, idealist, lover of life, is dead. His wife, two ex-wives and daughter gather for his funeral. As the true nature of the man and his life unfolds, these women discover much about themselves and the lives they have lived both within and outside his shadow. *Life After George* is a moving and perceptive insight into social change across three decades told through individual experiences. From the barricades of the student movements of the late 1960s to the new century with its demands for different educational strategies, the university has been central to change. And it is on this stage that George played out his brilliant, tempestuous career.

'*Life After George* is a comic drama guaranteed to restore your belief in the power of theatre.' Suzanne Brown—*Age*

2 Acts—2M, 4W

0 86819 628 2

Andrew Bovell/Hannie Rayson
SCENES FROM A SEPARATION
A fascinating collaboration between two of Australia's most talented writers which presents the male and female perspectives on a marriage. Mathew and Nina have been married for twelve years. He is forty—a successful publisher whose path is littered with the discarded souls of those who tried to keep up. Nina is thirty-eight and a journalist. She hasn't worked since the birth of the children. So when Mathew suggests she takes on the biography of Lawrence Clifford—tycoon, philanthropist and now Australian of the Year—she throws herself into the project with an all-consuming enthusiasm. A play about love, betrayal and sex, and about falling in love and getting found out.
2 Parts—3M, 4W
0 86819 476 X

CURRENCY MINI DRAMAS

This is a new series of plays by writers from all over Australia, suitable for students, amateur groups and anyone interested in exciting contemporary plays.

From a moving story of migrants negotiating new cultures to an inspiring account of an Aboriginal family surviving white paternalism ... from a black comedy-thriller to a futuristic nightmare ... and even a funny absurdist tale about fear of the unknown ... this series offers readers diversity, entertainment and a host of challenging ideas to explore.

Titles available:

Opening a Fuzzwollop's Frame of Mind by Daniel Evans
Mercy Thieves by Mark Kilmurry
Wild Rice by Huong Nguyen, Phi Hai, Pat Rix and Geoff Crowhurst
Last Chance Gas by Steve Taylor and Kevin Densley
Aliwa! by Dallas Winmar

For a full list of our titles, visit our website:
www.currency.com.au

Currency Press
The performing arts publisher
PO Box 2287
Strawberry Hills NSW 2012
Australia

Tel: (02) 9319 5877
Fax: (02) 9319 3649
Email: enquiries@currency.com.au

www.ingramcontent.com/pod-product-compliance
Lightning Source LLC
Chambersburg PA
CBHW041930090426
42744CB00017B/2004